COLLECTED WRITINGS ON ...

EXPLORING BIBLICAL HOLINESS

HAYES PRESS

Copyright © Hayes Press 2016

All rights reserved. No part of this book may be reproduced, stored in a retrieval system, or transmitted in any form, without the written permission of Hayes Press.

Published by:

HAYES PRESS Publisher, Resources & Media,

The Barn, Flaxlands

Royal Wootton Bassett

Swindon, SN4 8DY

United Kingdom

www.hayespress.org

Unless otherwise indicated, all Scripture quotations are from the Revised Version Bible (1885, Public Domain). Scriptures marked NKJV are from the HOLY BIBLE, the New King James Version® (NKJV®). Copyright © 1982 Thomas Nelson, Inc. Used by permission. All rights reserved." Scriptures marked NIV are from New International Version®, NIV® Copyright © 1973, 1978, 1984, 2011 by Biblica, Inc.™ Used by permission. All rights reserved worldwide. Scriptures marked

NASB are from the New American Standard Bible®, Copyright © 1960, 1962, 1963, 1968, 1971, 1972, 1973, 1975, 1977, 1995 by The Lockman Foundation. Used by permission (www.Lockman.org).

CHAPTER ONE: GOD, GLORIOUS IN HOLINESS (CRAIG JONES)

Any approach to this great subject must of necessity be in a spirit of humility and awe, sensing that as we draw near we are indeed treading 'holy ground'. This is a subject of profound depth, and its fullest reality lies beyond our total comprehension. However, spending time studying and considering the holiness of God is well spent, for we are bound as a result to be more aware of the awesomeness of God's holiness. So, realizing we are but looking at the tip of the iceberg, let us consider Moses' question in Exodus 15:11, "Who is like You, O LORD, among the gods? Who is like You, glorious in holiness, fearful in praises, doing wonders?"

Even a 'casual' glance through the Old Testament will give us a clear impression of the centrality and importance of the holiness of God in all Scripture and in all His dealings with His creation. The unfolding of God's purposes with chosen individuals to begin with, and eventually with a chosen nation, is so inextricably linked to impressing upon them, and subsequently upon us, the nature of God's holiness. From Abraham to Moses and the establishment of the holy nation of Israel, the message of God's holiness rings out.

All the furnishings, ordinances and trappings of the Tabernacle service were to speak of God's holiness from different perspectives, summed up by the words of God Himself in Leviticus

11:44, "you shall be holy, for I am holy". A count of the number of times the word 'holy' is used in the Pentateuch will underline this for us! And all that was but a foreshadowing of "the greater and more perfect tabernacle not made with hands, that is, not of this creation" (Heb.9:11). The supreme reason for their being called to holiness in every aspect of their lives was because Jehovah, glorious in holiness was in their midst, in the most holy place of the Tabernacle. So all of God's dealings through the Old Testament, the Tabernacle era, the Temple era, through the captivity and into the New Testament and from there into this present dispensation, have to do with, or emanate from, the essential holiness of God's character and nature.

It is very important that we try and grasp something of the intrinsic and absolute holiness of God, if we are to understand and appreciate more fully just how and why He deals with us in the way He does and how, in view of such things, we should live our lives in service for Him. A brief outline of the meanings of the main words used in Scripture for 'holy' or 'holiness' will be helpful at this point.

The most commonly used word rendered 'holy' in the Old Testament is the Hebrew word 'quodesh'. This essentially means 'a sacred place or thing' and may also convey the thought of being consecrated, dedicated or hallowed, especially in regard to God. This is the word used in Exodus 15:11. A related word is 'qadowsh', which conveys the sense of the absolute and intrinsic, characteristic holiness of God, both spiritually and morally (see 1 Sam.2:2; Hos.11:9).

There is a uniqueness in this aspect of God's holiness, for it sets Him apart, far above all that is created. There is a majesty in it too, which humbles us when we consider His glory shown in all creation around. Consider Isaiah 40:21-26, describing God's supremacy over all things, His creatorial power, then try and answer His question, "'To whom then will you liken Me, or to whom shall I be equal?' says the Holy One" (v.25). The only answer we can give is, "There is none like You, Lord God!" Indeed one may well be constrained, when contemplating God's majesty and holiness, to bow down and prostrate oneself in humble worship, in the spirit of the psalmist, and say, "Oh come, let us worship and bow down; let us kneel before the LORD our Maker" (Ps.95:6).

In the New Testament, the Greek word 'hagios' is most frequently used, indicating an intrinsic purity, sacredness and freedom from any defilement. Again, this would relate more to the absolute nature and character of God. 1 John 1:5 categorically states that "God is light and in Him is no darkness at all". Scripture clearly declares that "He is coming to judge the earth. With righteousness He shall judge the world, and the peoples with equity" (Ps.98:9), and that "a scepter of righteousness is the sceptre of Your kingdom" (Ps.45:6). We must be clear then; God is absolutely holy, therefore His righteousness is absolute, His judgement perfect and consequently, His condemnation of sin in us is just.

And yet His provision for our forgiveness through Christ's atoning death meets so wonderfully the exacting demands of His judgement for sin, and so we can be completely confident and assured in our faith in Christ, that since He paid the price on our behalf "There is therefore now no condemnation to those who are in Christ Jesus" (Rom.8:1).

If we needed further evidence of the truth of God's absolute holiness, we would be helped by considering some of the titles ascribed to Him, and how He is regarded by those angelic beings that minister to Him in heaven, and also by considering the nature of His dwelling place. It is sufficient for this purpose to let Scripture speak for itself; Isaiah 40:25 - 'the Holy One', Ezekiel 39:7 - 'I am the LORD, the Holy One in Israel', Revelation 4:8 - 'Holy, holy, holy. Lord God Almighty'. These are all summed up magnificently in Isaiah 57:15, "For thus says the High and Lofty One who inhabits eternity, whose name is Holy: 'I dwell in the high and holy place, with him who has a contrite and humble spirit, to revive the spirit of the humble, and to revive the heart of the contrite ones'"; which brings us to the matter of the implication of all this in our lives today.

Though our God is indeed the high and lofty One, dwelling in unapproachable light, glorious in holiness and majesty, the truth is that by His grace we do have access into His holy presence, individually and collectively. Having realized and appreciated afresh the holiness of God, then our approach to Him, though bold on the basis of Christ's work, is one of humility. We should ever be aware that to come into His presence is an awesome thing and it is incumbent upon us to approach Him appropriately. It is often said of the nature of true worship that bodily posture should reflect the feeling of the heart. We are called to be holy, just as He is holy, and our model, or example, is the Lord Jesus. He Himself demonstrated His own holiness throughout His life, not least by His unswerving dedication and obedience to His God and Father. We must strive for holiness too, as we endeavour to present our bodies "a living sacrifice, holy, acceptable to God, which is (our) reasonable service" (Rom.12:1).

Biblical quotations are from the NKJV.

CHAPTER TWO: JESUS, THE HOLY AND RIGHTEOUS ONE (PHIL KENNEDY)

How shall we describe the holiness and righteousness of the Son of God, except by reference to its capacity to excite self-revulsion, fear and powerlessness in those who encountered it? Isaiah, confronted with the burning holiness of the LORD of hosts, was filled with dread as he realized his own contemptible condition. Simon Peter was so overwhelmed by a sudden appreciation of his Master's singular holiness that he fell to his knees, imploring, 'Depart from me; for I am a sinful man, O Lord' (Lk.5:8). The aged apostle John fell as if dead at the feet of the glorified Christ, whom he described further as "he that is holy, he that is true" (Rev.3:7).

Isaiah saw Christ's pre-incarnate glory (Is.6:1-3; Jn.12:41), and as indicated by the acclaim of the seraphim, He was 'glorious in holiness'. When the prophet saw the Lord of hosts, he bewailed his 'unclean lips' and those of his people. Why unclean lips? Probably Isaiah had been struck by the abject state of Judah's leper king, for the vision belongs to 'the year that king Uzziah died'. Uzziah was made leprous on account of his presumptuous sin (2 Chron.26:21), and as a leper was required by the Law to cover his upper lip, and cry, 'Unclean, unclean!' (Lev.13:45). With great clarity Isaiah now perceived his own leper-like condition before the Holy One on the throne. How needy he and his people were, a people of unclean lips; how much in need of the One of whom it is written 'neither was guile found in his mouth'! (1 Pet.2:22).

The holiness and righteousness of Christ were neither imputed nor imparted, but intrinsic; they are qualities which are an essential part of the Son's eternal nature, and which the Father also carefully preserved throughout the days of His flesh. Sanctified in the eternal realm, and sent into the world (Jn.10:36), the Son would remain the Holy and Righteous One despite the pervasive presence of sin. In the secret hidden depths of 'the lowest parts of the earth', an expression which conveys both the womb symbolically (Ps.139:15) and the grave literally (Eph.4:9), nothing spoiled the holy flesh of the Son of God. Through the means of Holy Spirit conception, and the virgin birth, the Baby which Mary delivered was born holy (Lk.1:35).

The holy state of the Son was preserved despite the fact that every other infant has been 'shapen in iniquity' and conceived in sin (Ps.51:5). In death too, the holiness of His flesh was preserved, within that new tomb, which no man's dead body had defiled, the psalmist's prophecy had fulfilment, for no corruption could work in the body of God's holy One (Greek: 'hosios' - religiously right, unpolluted according to Strong and Vine) (Acts 2:26-32). We who have hoped in Christ shall 'put on' incorruptibility in resurrection (1 Cor.15:53), but in His deity He is 'the King eternal, incorruptible' (1 Tim.1:17). For us defilement and the need for cleansing can occur in both our flesh and our spirit (2 Cor.7:1). To Jesus uniquely belongs the spirit of holiness, marking Him out as the Son of God (Rom.1:4). He was One perfectly 'holy both in body and in spirit' (1

Cor.7:34), a sanctification which expressed itself in His being careful always for the things of His Father.

Christ was holy, that is, separated from sin and consecrated to God. The manner He lived that separated and consecrated life is worth considering. The Lord manifestly practised and exemplified His own teaching: "There is nothing from without the man, that going into him can defile him" (Mk.7:15). Contrary to the thought of the Pharisee, the profuse kisses of a harlot upon the feet of the Lord did not impugn His holiness (Lk.7:36-39). He was the friend of publicans and sinners without ever being compromised as to His own behaviour. His hand touched the leper man (Matt.8:3); the fevered hand of Peter's mother-in-law (Matt.8:15); the diseased eyes of the blind (Matt.9:29; 20:34); the ears and tongue of the deaf man with the speech impediment (Mk.7:33); and the bier that bore the body of the widow's son (Lk.7:14). Even the shame and spittle of His abusers could not detract in the smallest way from the intense white holiness which belonged to the Man from heaven. 'His life was pure, without a spot, And all His nature clean' expressed the poet. There was no trace in His mouth of any unwholesomeness of heart. Out of the heart of others 'come forth evil thoughts, murders, adulteries, fornications, thefts, false witness, railings: these are the things which defile the man' (Matt.15:19,20).

Devoid of such things, the mind, heart and mouth of Christ were undefiled. He is ever 'holy (Greek: hosios), guileless, undefiled' (Heb.7:26). The unclean spirits who encountered Christ recoiled from this unwavering holiness (Mk.1:23-27). They recognized it immediately, so diametrically opposite was it to their own nature. The unclean spirit in the man in the Capernaum synagogue sought to propound the demonic lie that the holiness of Christ among men must signify man's doom; hence the man's pit-inspired question, 'What have we to do with thee, thou Jesus of Nazareth? Art thou come to destroy us?' However, the Holy One of God had not drawn near to destroy human lives, but rather to save them. His holiness was the prerequisite of our salvation, for only by reason of His separateness from sinners in this respect could He die for their cleansing.

Yet one day that same holiness will require that all who die un-cleansed from their filthiness be for ever excluded from the presence of God and of the Lamb (Rev.22:11,15). What was patent to the unclean spirits is not always apparent to us: it is a matter for human belief. The unclean spirit with hostility and hopelessness said, 'I know thee ... the Holy One of God'. Simon Peter, however, was graciously allowed to cleave to the One who had words of eternal life to give him, stating "we have believed and know that thou art the Holy One of God" (Jn.6:69).

But even believing who He is does not necessarily impart the fear, the holy dread at what He is in His holiness. On the shore of Lake Gennesaret, Simon Peter and his companions were amazed by the miracle of the great catch of fish. They knew that a Man who was a sinner could not have worked such a sign. Peter fell down in sudden fear, confessing his own depravity and unworthiness to be with the Lord, until the Lord assured him of His grace towards him. But if we are to be companions of the Holy One, that grace must not be received in vain. 'Like as he which called you is holy, be ye yourselves also holy', Peter wrote later to the churches of the Diaspora (1 Pet.1:15). At times we also may become more acutely conscious of the tremendous difference between ourselves and the Lord; a difference not merely of degree but of essence.

In Spirit-led meditation, we have the veil pulled away for a glimpse of that glorious righteousness. We tremble at how far short we fall, till our holy Lord tells us our iniquity has been removed, and our sin expiated. He tells us, as He did Peter and John, 'Fear not'. He commissions us for service, having overcome our fear and defilement, and makes us fit to carry the message of the gospel. The natural man will not stay to contemplate this holiness. His instinct is to flee from the light, in case his evil works are reproved. Thus the men of Israel denied the Holy and Righteous One, preferring that they be granted a murderer (Acts 3:14). There was collusion among Gentile and Jew, Herod and Pontius Pilate, to destroy the One whom the Father had sanctified. For jealousy's sake, they were determined to crucify the anointed and obedient One, but God had anointed Him even for the death of the Cross.

On the Cross, 'him who knew no sin' - the truth put in negative form to help us more appreciate the positive attribute of holiness – "he made to be sin on our behalf, that we might become the righteousness of God in him" (2 Cor.5:21). Nothing was more foreign to the Holy and Righteous One than sin, Christ was not only righteous, but a lover of righteousness and who hated iniquity (Heb.1:9). No wonder that to Him the God-appointed experience of the Cross was one of 'deep mire' (Ps.69:2,14); the 'horrible pit'; and the 'miry clay' (Ps.40:2). At Golgotha the Holy One was made sin; the righteous servant bore the iniquities of many (Isa.53:11); and the Son's anguished cries went unanswered because of the holiness of His God (Ps.22:2,3). But the offering of that holy body was the all-sufficient basis for the sanctification of the people of God (Heb.10:10).

His steps were holy steps, and we are called to follow them (1 Pet.2:21,22). In this world He did no sin, and we must cease from it. There was no guile found in His mouth, and we must learn to speak truth with our neighbour. In death, Christ bore our sins in His holy body so that in life we might present our bodies "a living sacrifice, holy, acceptable to God" (Rom.12:2). For sanctified ones He has marked out a way: "it shall be called the way of holiness" (Is.35:8).

CHAPTER THREE: BE HOLY, FOR I AM HOLY (ROBERT SHAW)

Holiness belongs first of all to the nature of God. Three times over in Psalm 99 we are reminded that God is holy. The seraphim attending the throne of God, in awe and reverence and with the posture of worshippers in adoration, say, 'Holy, holy, holy is the LORD of hosts' (Is.6:3). Equally, the four living creatures of Revelation 4:8 have no rest day and night saying, 'Holy, holy, holy is the Lord God, the Almighty'. The threefold repetition of 'holy' is a Hebrew way of expressing transcendance or that God's holiness is absolute.

Its Beauty

Holiness is the perfect blending or harmony of virtues to form wholeness. There is no imbalance, no flaw, no fault, neither excess nor deficiency. As power is an expression of strength, so holiness is an expression of beauty. Ps.29:2 talks about the beauty of holiness. Holiness on display shows untarnished purity, unbending truth and limitless love. Such evidence is clearly seen in the life of Christ. Luke writes, 'that which is to be born shall be called holy, the Son of God' (Lk.1:35). Mark recites the confession of an unclean spirit, 'I know thee who thou art, the Holy One of God' (Mk.1:24). The writer to the Hebrews outlines His sanctified life as 'holy, guileless, undefiled, separated from sinners' (Heb.7:26).

Its Command

That God called His people to holiness, collectively and individually, is undeniable. Indeed, it was a requirement for His people. 'Be ye holy' is commanded by God to Israel several times in the book of Leviticus. The great importance God attaches to the subject is emphasized by the fact that the words 'holy' are mentioned about 200 times in the books of Exodus and Leviticus alone. Nadab and Abihu, two of Aaron's sons offered unauthorized and therefore unholy fire and died as a result. How awesome! God stated at that time a principle that exists for ever that all who serve Him must respect His holiness (Lev.10:3,10).

Peter declared in his first epistle, 'like as he which called you is holy, be ye yourselves also holy in all manner of living; because it is written, Ye shall be holy; for I am holy' (1 Pet.1:15,16).

Imputed Holiness

We know that there is within the believer the evidence of two natures. John says in the first chapter of his first epistle, 'If we say that we have no sin, we deceive ourselves, and the truth is not in us. If we confess our sins, he is faithful and righteous to forgive us our sins, and to cleanse us from all unrighteousness' (v.8,9). Equally, John speaks of the evidence of the new nature in chapter 3 of the same epistle at verse 9, 'Whosoever is begotten of God doeth no sin ... and he cannot sin, because he is begotten of God'.

It is true that holiness and sanctification are very similar terms and that scripture makes plain that we have been sanctified in

Christ Jesus (1 Cor.1:2,30). This is our happy state through the work of Christ at Calvary and our acceptance of Him as Saviour. Nothing can mar this imputed holiness. It is eternal. A. Wardle's hymn that refers so beautifully to holiness touches the point exactly:

"Thou, holy everlasting Cod,

Didst sanctify us by the blood

Of Thy beloved Son.

Raised from the dust of earth are we

To be a priesthood unto Thee,

Made holy in that One."

Acquired Holiness

Now the outcome of this sanctification surely must be the yielding of ourselves and of our lives to God. It is our separation to God. In effect it is holiness. This we must do for ourselves. It involves obedience and leads to purity in thought and life: to do what is right.

It is the attitude of the believer consequent upon the blessings of becoming a child of God. In such a relationship it is essential to represent the Father's holy character. To do this positively and acceptably sometimes requires the Father's discipline or chastening 'that we may be partakers of his holiness' (Heb.12:10). "Let us cleanse ourselves from all defilement of flesh and spirit, perfecting holiness in the fear of God" (See

2 Cor.6:17-7:1). Spirit, soul and body are involved. Men cannot lift up holy hands unless they are holy men. Similarly, holy women will be evident by their modesty and subjection in all things and by their eager exercise in good works (1 Tim.2:8-15).

The Holy Spirit's Aid to Holiness

The Holy Spirit plays an essential part in cultivating holiness. He is indeed represented to us as the Holy Spirit of God. Once again we are indebted to the apostle John for the words, "ye have an anointing from the Holy One, and ye know all things ... his anointing teacheth you concerning all things, and is true" (1 Jn.2:20,27). One of His functions is to impart the holiness of God to us. He does this as He develops within us a Christlike character. This, of course, is different from gifts distributed among believers by the Holy Spirit.

This matter of developing holiness is expected of all: it is God's expectation of the life of the believer. Just as the husbandman comes to the fruit orchard expecting a rich harvest so God expects the fruit of the Spirit from our lives. As many apples come from the same tree as there are many aspects of the fruit of the Spirit (see Gal.5:22,23) but the same source. The external evidence of fruit is the result of internal working. Our right behavior results from instruction by the Holy Spirit. If we allow our conduct to be governed by Him we shall be able to conquer the sinful desires of the old nature. Paul wrote very heart-searching and instructive words to the Thessalonian Church when he said, "the God of peace himself sanctify you wholly; and may your spirit, soul and body be preserved entire, without blame at the coming of our Lord Jesus Christ" (1 Thess.5:23).

The Effect of Holiness

How, then, do we measure up? The more the believer appreciates the holiness of God the more he or she will become aware of the sinfulness of sin. When Isaiah saw the holiness of God he saw his own uncleanness. Christ said to His disciples, "Ye therefore shall be perfect (i.e.: complete, spiritually whole) as your heavenly Father is perfect" (Matt.5:48). Surely, high as it is, this must be the target. David asked the question in Psalm 15, "LORD ... who shall dwell in thy holy hill?' His answer is a real challenge to every child of God because he sets out the qualifications of unimpeachable behaviour, doing and saying what is right, loving friends and neighbours, hating evil, being caring and careful and not seeking unjust gain. This catalogue of righteousness often catches us short.

"More purity give me, more strength to o'ercome;

More freedom from earthstains, more longings for home.

More fit for the kingdom, more used would I be,

More blessed and holy; more, Saviour, like Thee."

P.P. Bliss

CHAPTER FOUR: HOLINESS AND SEPARATION (ED NEELY)

Pharaoh spoke the truth when he first refused to allow the separation of Israel when Moses requested it. "I do not know the LORD ..." Separation and holiness are part of the essential character of God and are enjoined upon all who know Him; those who do not know Him will find the ideal not only intolerable, but impossible (1 Pet.1:16; Heb.12:14).

The principles of separation are taught from Genesis 1 to Revelation 22; holiness is first mentioned in relation to the calling out of a people for God. As God called Moses for the task of leading out this people, He set the standard by allowing Moses to stand on holy ground, but only on the basis of Moses emptying himself of self and personal authority, and giving complete obedience to the command of God (Ex.3:5). God's self-revelation to and in a nation demanded their separation: "Let My people go, that they may serve Me ..." What was true of Israel is also true today of a nation called out of darkness into light. He who rejects that separation, answers m the same measure as Pharaoh, "I do not know the Lord".

Ten times scripture states that Pharaoh hardened his heart, and ten times that God hardened it. But God waited until the king had hardened his own heart seven times before He first hardened it, though God in foreknowledge had predicted that this would be so. Indeed, God had raised him up so that divine power might be demonstrated in him (Rom.9:17). Yet the fact remains that it was in hardness of heart that Pharaoh rebelled against the purposes of God. Hardness of heart still wars against the separation that God desires for His people.

Pharaoh's claims that sacrifice is laziness, and that the miracles of men could explain away the miracles of God, couldn't convince even his own people (Ex.8:19; 10:7), yet he continued in his lies, mock-repentance and bravado, and decided that compromise must be the eventual answer. Poor Pharaoh - there is no compromise with God. Had Israel learned this earlier, they too might have been spared much of their torment under Pharaoh's hand (Ezek.20:8): Israel's idolatry in Egypt showed their unwillingness to trust God completely: "Then I resolved to pour out My wrath upon them, to accomplish My anger against them in the midst of the land of Egypt." The believer in Christ will also greatly benefit from learning that same lesson early.

The fact that God had made a division between the Egyptians and the children of Israel in the land of Egypt (Ex.8:22 ff), was not sufficient reason to compromise by sacrificing to God within the land (Ex.9:25,26). Apart altogether from the obvious, that such sacrifices could only be misunderstood and obnoxious to the Egyptians, God had commanded the separation of His people (Ex.8:26,27). Present day collective service demands a similar type of separation (Heb.13:12-15). The prophecy of Hosea 11:1, fulfilled in Christ (Matt.2:15), still calls for obedient response in the hearts and lives of those who would live godly lives: "Out of Egypt I called My Son".

Nor would separation with strings attached answer the command. "Don't go far away" (see Ex.8:28), is still the cry of a world that has yet to learn that righteousness and lawlessness have no partnership; light and darkness no fellowship; Christ and Belial no harmony. "Come out from their midst and be separate" says the Lord. "And do not touch what is unclean; And I will welcome you. And I will be a Father to you, and you shall be sons and daughters to Me" (2 Cor.6:14-18). Not far away? The command to separate from, and separate to, is total and absolute. That only some should go, or that possessions be left behind, must be answered with resolve and fulfilment: "not a hoof will be left behind". Furthermore, when God brought them out they would not go empty. The night of their separation is described as "for the LORD" (Ex.12:42). He would bring them out and bring them in full. Their continuation in that fulness and the enjoyment of it would depend on continued political, connubial, and ecclesiastical separation.

Today, right thinking believers in the Lord Jesus Christ have no difficulty in seeing the necessity for separation from the grosser evils of this world. Difficulty sometimes arises, however, in discerning the need for separation in areas where we could seemingly benefit or be a benefit politics, marriage, religious affiliation. The warnings of Deuteronomy 7 are the claims of God, not Moses: "For you are a holy people to the LORD your God; the LORD your God has chosen you to be a people for His own possession out of all peoples who are on the face of the earth ... Therefore, you shall keep the commandment and the statutes which I am commanding you today, to do them" (vv. 6,11).

No covenants, no favour in judgement, no intermarriage, no trying to reform the wrong religious worship - separation was to bring spiritual, physical, economic blessing beyond anything that they could imagine; less than separation would cause the nation to perish (8:19). God's standards have not changed in our dispensation. We are in the world and submissive to its authorities (Jn.17:15-18; 1 Pet.2:13-17), yet not of it and its ambitions and pleasures. Not only so, but spiritual enlightenment is a progressive thing and does not allow of a return to a degree darkness which at the time meant a measure of light to us: "For if I rebuild what I have once destroyed, I prove myself to be a transgressor" (Gal.2:18).

We never cease to be one with fellow members of the Body of Christ, but separation from practices inconsistent with the revelation of divine truth to us is ever taught in the New Testament, and involves separation, therefore, from people who are believers also. In the ultimate, this may even necessitate separation from some who are within churches of God, as censure and discipline are carried out according to divine directions (Rom.16:17; 1 Cor.5:11; 2 Thess.3:6). If such is enjoined even within the holy nation, have we difficulty with the principles of separation from those without? Separation in itself does not involve enmity as 2 Thessalonians 3:14,15 clearly shows. This was illustrated in Israel's experience in Deuteronomy 2:5,9: Israel were brothers with Edom and Moab and were not to be jealous of God's blessings upon them nor envious nor covetous of their possessions. Israel turned away rather than engage in battle with them and took the long way around rather than vex those who also had received God's blessings. God would later show the principle - them that are without, God judges (1 Cor.5:13).

Balaam, with eyes wide open, enlightened by the Lord, saw God's vision of His people: "As I see him from the tops of the rocks, and I look at him from the hills; Behold, a people who dwells apart, and shall not be reckoned among the nations" (Num.23:9). Who among God's people would have it otherwise? Isaiah says: "The nations are like a drop from a bucket, and are regarded as a speck of dust on the scales ... All the nations are as nothing before Him, they are regarded as less than nothing and meaningless" (Is.40:15,17). But: "you are a chosen race, a royal priesthood, a Holy Nation, a people for God's own possession ... you are the people of God" (1 Pet.2:9-10).

The importance of the nation that God chooses is underscored in the remarkable words of Deuteronomy 32:8,9: "When the Most High gave the nations their inheritance, when He separated the sons of man, He set the boundaries of the peoples according to the number of the sons of Israel. For the LORD's portion is His people." And: "Christ Jesus ... gave Himself for us, that He might redeem us from every lawless deed and purify for Himself a people for His own possession ..." (Tit.2:14).

A promise of blessings and curses followed God's call to Israel, each dependent upon the measure of obedience of the people to God's commandments. The checkered history of the nation proved the accuracy of divine promise. The history of God's dealings with the early churches of the New Testament is a re-statement of God's fidelity to His word. God will not be unfaithful to His word in our day either. Holiness and separation will bring blessing; and hidden manna, a white stone, and a place on the throne of Christ are still offered to the overcomer (Rev.2:17; 3:21). And to such as are otherwise, the promise of tribulation and pestilence and a spewing from the mouth of God. God's will is to dwell among a separated and holy people; a people who in every sense of the word "know the Lord". "I will dwell in them and walk among them; and I will be their God, and they shall be My people. Therefore, come out ... and be separate ... perfecting holiness in the fear of God (2 Cor.6:16-7:1).

CHAPTER FIVE: THE WORK OF THE HOLY SPIRIT (ROY DICKSON)

"grieve not the Holy Spirit of God in whom ye were sealed unto the day of redemption" (Eph.4:30). This single verse reminds us of so much scriptural truth. We learn that the Holy Spirit is Deity and that He is a Person. We also learn here that we are sealed in Him unto the day of our redemption; we cannot, therefore, lose our salvation. Praise God! The whole point of the verse is, however, that we are not to grieve, in the sense of causing anguish to this gracious, indwelling Person of the Godhead.

'... grieve not the Holy Spirit' - Such a request would not be made unless there was the possibility that we could grieve Him and unless God had provided a way of escape from falling into this sad situation (1 Cor.10:13). It is with this backdrop that we approach the work of the Holy Spirit in this chapter. Holiness is a word which is almost devoid of meaning now as far as the lifestyle of many people is concerned; in fact, the word has connotations of monastic-like seclusion which makes it appear outdated for this century, in which sensuality in all forms prevails in modern thinking.

Christian, look again. Holiness applies to us, even in this era in which God has placed us "... upon whom the ends of the ages are come" (1 Cor.10:11). Be certain of this, we are in the front line of the battle, and God places tremendous importance on holiness, for He "... saved us, and called us with a holy calling' (2 Tim.1:9). Remember, firstly, that when we believed we received the Spirit being baptized by the Lord Jesus into the Body of Christ (1 Cor.12:13). Those who receive the Spirit are called 'saints' (Rom.1:7) and the lives of saints of God are to be characterized by holiness. Questions immediately arise. What does being holy mean? How do I become holy? Is there a standard I must aim for? Let us consider some of these.

Thank God for lavishing His Spirit upon us! This means that we need not try to achieve holiness as an impossible quest or as an optional extra to our Christianity. The Spirit is within us and we are sealed in Him, so that we should be empowered to know the reality of holiness. As the Spirit is holy, so He wants us to be holy in our moral and spiritual lives, publicly and privately. It is a recurring theme of Scripture that God desires those who love Him to be overcomers, not allowing the corruption of the world to pervade their hearts and minds. We see this theme coming through what the Spirit says to the churches: "But thou hast a few names in Sardis which did not defile their garments: and they shall walk with me in white; for they are worthy. He that overcometh shall thus be arrayed in white garments; and I will in no wise blot his name out of the book of life" (Rev.3:4,5).

Yes, God desires that as children of God, we should strive to be overcomers (Rom.8:37). It is the difference between being "fashioned according to this world" (Rom.12:2) and being "transformed into the same image" i.e. of His Son (2 Cor.3:18). It is only by the power of the indwelling Holy Spirit that we can be transformed into the image of Christ; for He, the Spirit, is "the Spirit of Christ" (Rom.8:9) and as the Spirit is holy so are we to be, for He is within us. Moreover, He will not leave us even though, sadly, on occasion we do grieve Him. A beautiful expression which may help us to capture in our thoughts what God's purpose is for our transformed lives is given in 2 Thessalonians 2:13 and 1 Peter 1:2 where we read in both verses "... in sanctification of the Spirit".

These verses both reveal that God the Father knew all about us long before we were born and He chose us for sanctification in His Spirit by His own sovereign grace. This expression should really stop us in our tracks and cause us to reflect, for God has set us apart (sanctified) in the Holy Spirit so that His marvellous purposes in us might be fulfilled not thwarted. Of course, God's eternal purposes will be fulfilled because His Word declares it (Is.14:24), but there is no certainty that as individuals we will radiate God's love and holiness. What sadness if we grieve or quench (1 Thess.5:19) the Spirit to the point where this sanctification of the Spirit is not seen in our lives.

Surely, this setting apart of our lives by God for sanctification in His Holy Spirit should encourage us to know more fully God's will for us and to learn how we can walk by the Spirit (Gal.5:16) and be overcomers. The power of the blood of Christ enables us to overcome, and the Devil's accusations against us (Rev.12:10) fail when we claim this supreme power. This is crucial to our daily victory over sin, for just as the blood of Jesus cleanses us from all sin (1 Jn.1:7) so Christ has also "... loosed us from our sins by His blood" (Rev.1:5). The same thought is contained in Romans 6:8-11. This means that we are to consider ourselves as set free from the dominion of sin in our lives. This is a here and now possibility, demonstrating before others the reality of Christ's atoning death and victorious resurrection. We can experience victory over sin's power day by day.

Fellow believer, let us together lay hold on this fact that God, from before the beginning of creation, set us apart for sanctification in His Spirit and He has given us the means by virtue of the indwelling Spirit to realize progressively His power in our lives and so to walk in holiness. Is He, the gracious Spirit, an untapped resource in your struggle with the 'old man' (Col.3:8,9) within you? Indeed, do you struggle with your old nature or does it rule the day? That's not what God wants of us. Paul knew all about this struggle, the new nature born of the Spirit by the incorruptible Word of God (1 Pet.1:23) battling against the tendency of the old. Read about it in Romans 7:14-25.

Our tendency to sin cannot be overcome by 'trying that bit harder' or by denying ourselves: human effort and abstinence cannot defeat the power of sin. Paul wrote in Romans 8:9, "But ye are not in the flesh, but in the Spirit, if so be that the Spirit of God dwelleth in you". How can we know, therefore, this experience of victory over the power of sin in our mortal bodies? We shall consider this more fully in the next chapter, but perhaps a pointer is given by John the Baptist after he had seen the Lord, "He must increase, but I must decrease" (Jn.3:30).

The problem so often stems from love of self, stifling our love of Christ which should be evident in our lives. The Spirit of God is given to help us. He has been given a wonderful mission by God to fulfil in the lives of those who are born again. That mission is to form the image of Christ in each believer, so that not only might we be 'in Christ' (Eph.1:1) as members of His Body (1 Cor.12:27), but also grown into His likeness. We can see this in Paul's great discourse in Romans where, having argued that we have received new life through the Spirit (Rom.8:11), he goes on to show that those who have the Spirit are to mortify the deeds of the body (Rom.8:13). "For as many as are led by the Spirit of God, these are sons of God" (Rom.8:14).

"But we are children of God," you might say, "because we have been born again". True, but in Romans 8 there is the possibility of becoming sons of God. The difference? The difference is that those who are sons are like the Father in character. Note what the Lord said to Philip, "He that hath seen me hath seen the Father" (Jn.14:9). In character the Father, the Son and the Holy Spirit are the same in holiness, and we, if we are led by the Spirit, will make it evident that we are sons of God. The Spirit does not wish to automate us for our God is not a God of forced entry, but of invitation, correction and ultimately, of sovereign grace.

Paul adds in Galatians 4:19, "My little children, of whom I am again in travail until Christ be formed in you". Read also, please, Galatians 5:22,23 and examine yourself and examine Christ against the fruit which a Spirit filled life produces. Here is our standard of holiness to aim for, even the Example of Christ. We cannot mix and match what we prefer from God's Word, or which aspects of the Spirit's working are most compatible with our natural self. So often our lives see-saw between 'more of me' and 'more of Christ' because the old nature, the flesh, troubles us so frequently. Christian, in order for you and me to grow in holiness we need to grow more like Christ in character and deed.

Together let us look only to Jesus (Heb.12:2) in our mind-set, and put on Christ (Rom.13:14) in our daily conduct, and by the faithful and diligent drinking in of God's Word, let us "... be filled with the Spirit" (Eph.5:18). Yes, we were indeed sanctified in the Spirit, as we have seen, by God in the timeless beginning, but sanctification is also to be followed after. For those who do, a wonderful promise of great spiritual value awaits to be fulfilled by a faithful God. A promise which we can grasp by faith; please read it in Hebrews 12:14 and also in Matthew 5:8. We do not yet see Him face to face, but as we are more and more transformed into His image, we shall enjoy ever closer communion with Him, and so by faith we shall "see the Lord". The indwelling Spirit strengthening us, fellow Christian, let us together "... follow after sanctification" (Heb.12:14).

CHAPTER SIX: HOLINESS AND LOVE (ALAN TOMS)

God called Jeremiah to be a prophet in the thirteenth year of the reign of king Josiah, who was quite a remarkable king. When he was sixteen years of age he began to seek God, and when he was twenty he campaigned against idolatry in his land (2 Chr.34:1-3).

A few years later the book of the law was found in God's house, and the reading of it so affected the king that his reforms became even more thorough (2 Chr.34:14,19). There was no doubt about his sincerity, but unfortunately it was not shared by his people. God said about them, "Judah hath not returned unto Me with her whole heart, bat feignedly" (Jer.3:10). There was change because Josiah insisted upon it, but it was not a change of heart and that was why Jeremiah's task was so difficult. But if the people were not speaking from their hearts, God certainly was, judging by some of the things He said through Jeremiah in the second chapter of his prophecy. Of the many questions that God asked perhaps the most striking is found in verse 5: "What unrighteousness have your fathers found in Me, that they are gone far from Me, and have walked after vanity, and are become vain?"

It is remarkable that God should ask such a question. Of course, it was calculated to bring them to the point where they acknowledged that there was no fault in God and never could be; then it would only be a tiny step for them to take to realize that the fault must be in them, but they never got that far. Patiently God pleaded with them - oh, how much He loved them - and looking back to the early days of their love for Him He said: "I remember for thee the kindness of thy youth, the love of thine espousals; how thou wentest after Me in the wilderness, in a land that was not sown" (v.2). How like the Lord that was, to give credit where it was due. He never forgot Israel's first love. They did not follow for what they got out of it. All around them was a barren land, and the going was hard. Obviously it was love for the Lord that drew them. That was true love, that follows out of regard for the Person rather than anything He gives. God took note of that and never forgot it.

The Lord Jesus put a searching question to Peter when He said, "Simon, son of John, lovest thou Me? It drew from Peter's heart the confession, "Yea, Lord; Thou knowest that I love Thee" (Jn.21:15). First love is a very precious thing. First love produces first works, but first love can fade. The heart can grow cold. That is what happened in Ephesus, and the Lord was caused to say: "But I have this against thee, that thou didst leave thy first love" (Rev.2:4).

The Lord remembers first love and first works, He never forgets. First love produces holy lives. It did that in Israel's case. "Israel was holiness unto the LORD" (v.3). The God who had called them was a holy God, and love for Him had produced holy lives on their part. Their hearts were true, their love was warm, their lives were pure, and their works were full of zeal. But in Jeremiah's day they had strayed far away, and God was pleading with them to tell Him why they had done so.

God had a complaint against His people; they had been unfaithful. They had turned away from His love to worthless idols and to all the sin and uncleanness that went with idol worship, but although He pleaded with them they refused to return to Him. The heart of God was sorely wounded: "Pass over to the Isles of Kittim and see; and send unto Kedar, and consider diligently; and see if there hath been such a thing. Hath a nation changed their gods, which yet are no gods? but My people have changed their Glory for that which doth not profit" (vv. 10,11).

His people had treated Him worse than the nations around Israel had treated their idols. The idol gods never demanded anything of their adherents which conflicted with their sinful desires; they could serve their gods and live as they pleased. Israel could not do that with God, and neither can we. Therein lies the great difference. Israel was holy to the Lord as long as their first love lasted, for the God who saved them was a holy God. "Ye shall be holy; for I am holy" is the divine requirement carried from the Old Testament into the New Testament (1 Pet.1:16). It is binding on us all, and in a world that is full of corruption and lust God calls us to lives that are holy and pure. Let us remember that God is looking for love that comes from a pure heart, a good conscience, and sincere faith (1 Tim.1:5). "Keep thyself pure" is His word to us all. "But flee youthful lusts, and follow after righteousness, faith, love, peace, with them that call on the Lord out of a pure heart" (2 Tim.2:22). The message comes to us all today. Soon our Master will return. Will He find our hearts beating true to Him when He comes?

CHAPTER SEVEN: THE FRUIT OF HOLINESS IN OUR LIVES (LINDSAY WOODS)

"You were taught, with regard to your former way of life, to put off your old self, which is being corrupted by its deceitful desires; to be made new in the attitude of your minds; and to put on the new self, created to be like God in true righteousness and holiness" (Eph.4:22-24 NIV).

The Call to Holiness

God has saved us and called us to Himself, so that we might glorify Him in our lives. The Westminster Catechism sums it up beautifully: 'Man's chief end is to glorify God and enjoy Him for ever'. In order to glorify God we must bear fruit, for Christ said to His disciples, "This is to my Father's glory, that you bear much fruit, showing yourselves to be my disciples" (Jn.15:8 NIV). The ultimate glory of God should be our greatest motivation in His service and for our supreme example and encouragement we look at the lovely life of the man Christ Jesus. He could say near the end of His life on earth, "I have brought you glory on earth by completing the work you gave me to do" (Jn.17:4 NIV). In all His life He was "... holy, blameless, pure, set apart from sinners" (Heb.7:26 NIV).

If we are to bear rich and plentiful fruit we shall need to learn the secret of abiding in Christ (Jn.15). He is the vine, we are the branches, and we shall not be fruitbearing branches unless we too are holy. In fact it is God's command "... Just as he who called you is holy, so be holy in all you do; for it is written: "Be holy, because I am holy" (1 Pet.1:15,16 NIV). Fruitfulness will result only from a disciplined life of feeding, nourishment and pruning. This is not an optional extra for us as Christians, but an absolute necessity for 'without holiness no-one will see the Lord' (Heb.12:14 NIV). Christ gives us a promise with a challenge when He says, 'Blessed are the pure in heart for they will see God' (Matt.5:8 NIV). The vine is full of health and vitality, 'for in him dwelleth all the fulness of the Godhead bodily' (Col.2:9), and if we are to grow to be fruitbearing branches we shall need to draw our energy and strength from Him.

"Our fellowship is with the Father and with his Son, Jesus Christ' (1 Jn.1:3), and as we experience this fellowship we become "partakers of his holiness" (Heb.12:10). When we first put our faith in Christ, we were taken out of our sins and put "in Christ"; as Paul says, "Christ in you, the hope of glory" (Col.1:27). As we grow and develop in our new life with Christ we should be experiencing what it means for Christ to be in us. Paul's prayer for the Ephesians was "that Christ may dwell in your hearts through faith" (3:17).

Holy Lives

God is serious about holiness in the lives of His people, and He will discipline us to attain it. Holiness and usefulness are linked together. We cannot bring our service to God in an unclean vessel. Paul says to Timothy, 'If a man cleanses himself from ... (ignoble purposes), he will be an instrument for noble purposes, made holy, useful to the Master and prepared to do any good work' (2 Tim.2:21 NIV). One of the surest evidences that we are in Christ is in the living of a holy life. A tree can be recognized by its fruit, for as the Lord explained in Matthew 7:16-20 "... do people pick grapes from thorn bushes, or figs from thistles? Likewise every good tree bears good fruit ... Thus, by their fruit you will recognise them" (NIV).

Good and evil come from our hearts (Lk.6:45) and out of the overflow of the heart the mouth speaks. The fruit of our lives is in what we say and do. How often do our hearts overflow, and how do we give expression to this overflowing in our assembly, family and secular lives? Is there a continual sacrifice of praise to God from our lives in "the fruit of lips that confess his name"? (Heb.13:15 NIV). James warns us of the very powerful influence for good and bad of the tongue: "Out of the same mouth come praise and cursing. My brothers, this should not be. Can both fresh water and salt water flow from the same spring? My brothers, can a fig-tree bear olives, or a grapevine bear figs?" (3:10-13 NIV). If we respond to Peter's exhortation "... sanctify in your hearts Christ as Lord" (1 Pet.3:15), then the spring will be fresh water, the tree will be good, and the inevitable fruit will be to His praise and glory (Eph.1:6,12,14).

God's call is to holiness that will bring Him and His Son eternal praise and glory, and He

knows that at the same time it will be for the highest quality of life for us, abundant life (Jn.10:10). The vinedresser prunes to increase fruitbearing; He takes away the unwanted growth and the dead wood because He loves us, and He wants us to produce the fruit of righteousness (Heb.12:4-11). At the time, pruning may seem painful and severe, but it is for our good and to His glory. If we go in for satisfying our carnal and natural appetites, which are the desires of our old nature, the flesh, then sadly its fruit will be seen in our lives: dead wood that must be removed and is only fit for burning.

In Galatians 5 there is a contrast between the works of the flesh and the fruit of the Spirit and there is no doubting what ought to be seen in our lives as new creatures in Christ "... love, joy, peace, patience, kindness, goodness, faithfulness, gentleness and self-control" (vv.22,23).

Holiness - A Personal Responsibility

This work of God will not be completed without us playing our part, for it is our serious responsibility to "cleanse ourselves from all defilement of flesh and spirit, perfecting holiness in the fear of God" (2 Cor.7:1). Of course this will not be achieved in our own strength, but such deep inner changes will be the work of Christ and the Holy Spirit as we submit and discipline our lives before Him; "... that out of his glorious riches he may strengthen you with power through his Spirit in your inner being" (Eph.3:16 NIV). Let us be encouraged for God "is able to do immeasurably more than all we ask or imagine, according to his power that is at work within us" (Eph.3:20 NIV).

Self-control: Fruit of the Spirit

The Holy Spirit will show us our sinfulness and the glory of God's holiness. Paul says, "... live by the Spirit, and you will not gratify the desires of the sinful nature" (Gal.5:16 NIV). The New Testament writers speak often of self-control because it is such an essential element of the Spirit's fruit. Peter encourages us to express godliness in: faith, goodness, knowledge, self-control, perseverance, godliness, brotherly kindness, love; so that we shall be kept "from being ineffective and unproductive in" our "knowledge of our Lord Jesus Christ" (2 Pet.1:5-8 NIV).

Self-control will begin in the mind, bringing 'every thought into captivity unto the obedience of Christ' (2 Cor.10:5) - controlling our own thoughts, and captivating the minds of others with our lifestyle and Christlikeness. 'The means to the transformed life is by the renewal of the mind. This means nothing more and nothing less than education, serious education. In-depth education. Disciplined education in the things of God. It calls for the mastery of the Word of God. We need to be people whose lives have changed because our minds have changed ... This is the call to excellence we have received'.*

Our responsibility is to guard our minds and emotions from unholy influences and desires. As we do our part, we will see the Spirit of God do His part in making us more holy. In this matter we will need to ask of God for heavenly wisdom which will produce a good life of humility, a life that is "pure, then peace loving, considerate, submissive, full of mercy and good fruit, impartial and sincere. Peacemakers who sow in peace raise a harvest of righteousness" (see James 3:13-18 NIV). Planted by the streams of water (Ps.1:3) that flow from the sanctuary to the fruit trees (Ezek.47:12) we will bear leaves that do not wither, and good fruit even into old age (Ps.92:13,14).

COLLECTED WRITINGS ON ... EXPLORING BIBLICAL HOLINESS

A life without holiness will be fruitless and such a disappointment to our holy God who gave His Servant Jesus to die for us: "For he chose us in him before the creation of the world to be holy and blameless in his sight" (Eph.1:3,4 NIV). Believers belong to Christ "who was raised from the dead, in order that we might bear fruit to God" (Rom.7:4 NIV). "May he strengthen your hearts so that you will be blameless and holy in the presence of our God and Father when our Lord Jesus comes with all his holy ones" (1 Thess.3:13 NIV).

*Quotations from The Pursuit of Holiness by Jerry Bridges.

CHAPTER EIGHT: HOLINESS BEFITTING GOD'S HOUSE (STEVE SEDDON)

Earlier chapters have led us through the truth of divine holiness clearly seen in the character of God revealed in His Word. A truth also profoundly demonstrated through the Person of the Lord Jesus in His declaration of His Father (Jn.1:18). We now turn our focus towards the place where God chooses to make His dwelling and see how this, God's house, must also be characterized by holiness.

A Dwelling Fit for God

"The Lord reigns, he is robed in majesty ... holiness adorns your house" (Ps.93:1,5). Where the NIV uses the word 'adorns', other versions refer to holiness 'befitting' or 'becoming' God's house. The underlying thought from the original Hebrew word is that for the holy God to dwell, or more literally, to feel 'at home' in His house, then holiness should be one of its characteristics. What makes a place holy? If we trace the origins of the house of God back through the Old Testament to the time when Jacob had his dream at Bethel, it is clear that holiness is something that must characterize any place where God had made His dwelling. Jacob awaking from his dream could declare, "How awesome is this place! This is none other than the house of God" (Gen.28:17 NIV).

Similarly it was Moses' experience at the burning bush that this place, by virtue of God's presence, was indeed 'holy ground' (Ex.3:5). The point we are making is this: when it comes to God's chosen dwelling place, it is above all else. His presence which makes the place holy. However, as we follow the development of God's house, it is clear that certain characteristics of the house: its structure, the materials from which it was built, who served in the house and how they served, must be of a standard that is appropriate for the dwelling of the holy God. Holiness must 'adorn' every aspect of His house.

A Holy House

If we look at God's dwelling place in the Old Testament tabernacle, we see a structure which had been made absolutely in accordance with God's own pattern (Ex.25:9). It was made of precious materials chosen by God (Ex.35:5-9), and offered willingly by His people (Ex.35:21). So we see a clear parallel in God's chosen dwelling place today - a spiritual house. It is a building made from chosen materials, in fact living stones (1 Pet.2:5), being assembled in accordance with a divine pattern (Eph.2:21,22). However, the holiness associated with God's house both in the Old Testament and now, goes beyond the structure of the building and its materials: holiness must also be characteristic of the behaviour of those who serve there.

A Holy Priesthood

God's judgement on Aaron's sons, Nadab and Abihu, was severe. They offered unauthorized sacrifices which were contrary to God's command and as a result were consumed by fire

(Lev.10). Clearly a holy God cannot tolerate services done in His holy sanctuary by priests who themselves are less than holy. The highest privilege today of those who serve in the house of God, is as 'a holy priesthood, offering spiritual sacrifices acceptable to God through Jesus Christ' (1 Pet.2:5 NIV) - a service we do collectively at the Remembrance.

However, as priests we should be exercised that our lives are consecrated to the service of God's house. The apostle Paul is very explicit in his instructions regarding our preparation for service of the holies, 'A man ought to examine himself before he eats of the bread and drinks of the cup' (1 Cor.11:28 NIV). The word 'examine' has strong implications: if we 'examine' something, we subject it, not to a cursory glance, but rather to meticulous scrutiny. Such an examination cannot be done in the last few minutes before the Remembrance starts, it must be an on-going daily exercise. Remember the lesson of the laver: the vessel in which the priests washed themselves before entering the holy place. It was made from mirrors.

Our daily exercise before God must be to look into the mirror of His Word, thereby exposing those blemishes in our character and behaviour which spoil our holiness. Our daily aspiration should be to see from God's Word the holy character of the Lord Jesus, and then by continuous cleansing, allow His holiness to be reflected in our behaviour. This must be the quality of our heart-searching before we conduct our holy priesthood service.

Collectively Holy

The believer on the Lord Jesus should be aware that his or her 'body is a temple of the Holy Spirit' (1 Cor.6:19) that is a dwelling place for the Spirit of God. The pursuit of personal holiness is essential if we are to experience His power and presence in our lives. However, while it is God's desire to dwell in individuals, it is also His longing to dwell among a collective group of people: "a chosen people, a royal priesthood, a holy nation, a people belonging to God, that you may declare the praises of him who called you out of darkness into his wonderful light' (1 Pet.2:9 NIV). It is therefore important that the holiness of God's people extends beyond the individual, and is seen to pervade their collective behaviour as local churches of God, and then further still, as a united collection of churches – "every building, fitly framed together" (Eph.2:21 RV margin) growing "into a holy temple in the Lord".

Paul was deeply concerned for the Church of God in Corinth, in particular the danger of associations with unbelievers which, however subtle, would compromise their holy, separated position. As a Church, he instructed them: "Do not be yoked together with unbelievers ... for we are the temple of the living God ... come out from them and be separate, says the Lord ... let us purify ourselves from everything that contaminates body and spirit, perfecting holiness out of reverence for God" (2 Cor.6:14-7:1 NIV). So we must also be on our guard that our holy separated position, as the people of God, is not compromised by improper associations with those who do not share our calling.

All for God

We ought not to lose sight of the purpose of our call to holiness in the context of our service in His house. It is for His pleasure that we have been called to be holy, individually, and collectively as His special people. "For the grace of God that brings salvation has appeared to all men. It teaches us to say 'No' to ungodliness and worldly passions, and to live self-controlled, upright and godly lives in this present age, while we wait for the blessed hope – the glorious appearing of our great God and Saviour, Jesus Christ, who gave himself for us to redeem us from all wickedness and to purify for himself a people that are his very own, eager to do what is good" (Tit.2:11-14 NIV).

May God bring us each a deeper appreciation of our privilege as "a people that are his very own", and as we delight in our privilege may He be glorified by the holiness which adorns His house. "Ascribe to the LORD the glory due to his name; worship the LORD in the splendour of his holiness" (Ps.29:2 NIV).

CHAPTER NINE: HOLINESS AND SANCTIFICATION (GUY JARVIE)

Holiness and sanctification are closely allied in the Scriptures. Holiness might be described as the result of sanctification, and sanctification is being "set apart." All believers are saints, that is, those whom God has sanctified, and as saints we ought to be saintly. We are commanded to be holy because God is holy (1 Pet.1:16).

In Exodus 19:5,6 God said that the people of Israel would be a holy nation if they would obey His voice and keep His covenant. They were to be a nation separate from all other nations. "Ye shall be holy unto Me: for I the LORD am holy, and have separated you from the peoples, that ye should be Mine" (Lev.20:26). Their history shows how often they fell far short of what they might and should have been.

But holiness, or separation to God, is costly, and in Leviticus 10:1-3 we find what the price of holiness was to Israel. God had separated Aaron and his sons to be holy, as those who came near to Him. But two of the sons of Aaron came near to God with strange fire, and fire came forth from the LORD and slew them. It was the price of holiness. They had failed to draw near to God as He had commanded, and this cost them their lives. Their fire was of their own kindling; it had not come from the altar which speaks of Christ. God is holy, and He will be sanctified in those who come near to Him. He is not to be served by fools or by the self-willed. We must serve in love and holy fear. Lest we should think that such judgement could not happen today, we have the example of Ananias and Sapphira, who died, because in lying to God's servants, they were really lying to God (Acts 5). Then we must remember the need for holiness as we draw near to take the bread and the wine, lest we come under judgement (1 Cor.11:27-29).

In John 17 we find the Lord Jesus praying to the Father, and in verse eleven He says, "Holy Father, keep them (the disciples) in Thy name which Thou hast given Me." God is a Father, with all the affection and care of which that word speaks, but He is a Holy Father. How careful then we must be in all our walk before Him! How careful must we be that we represent His holy character in our lives before others. In 1 Peter 1:14-19 we read that we should pass the time of our sojourning in fear. We should fear sin and all uncleanness. We shall appreciate the sinfulness of sin, only as we realize the holy character of God. It was when Isaiah saw the Lord, that He saw His own uncleanness, and so with us. As we think of His holy character, we will fear to harbour bitterness or pride, or uncleanness or deceit in our hearts. We must remember that the evil thoughts of the heart defile us (Mk. 7:20-28).

The Christian must be separate from the world so that he may be holy to the Lord. From the lust of the flesh, the lust of the eyes, and the vainglory of life, he must guard himself. He should eschew smoking, cinemas, and ostentation in dress, and from evil in any other form he must be separate. These are of the world, and they defile the servant of Christ. He is to be holy to his God.

Then also he is not to be unequally yoked with unbelievers (2 Cor.6:14,15). The Spirit of God will reveal to us the things from which we should separate. We can only have power with God and with men, as we separate from unclean things. It is important for us to see that holiness is related to the word of God. In Leviticus 11 we find that in the Old Testament an Israelite would be defiled if he ate certain kinds of flesh. Holiness demanded that he abstain from them. But this is not so in the New Testament, for the Lord Jesus has made all meats clean (Mk.7:19). So then holiness is dependent upon the word of the Lord to us. It is not dependent upon our feelings, nor upon the customs of the nations. Our customs must conform to God's word. Among the Chinese, blood is commonly used as a kind of sauce to be taken with food, but it must not be so used among Christians, because it is forbidden to the believer to eat blood (Acts 15:28,29).

In 1 Timothy 2.8 we read that men should pray in every place, lifting up holy hands, without wrath and disputing. Holy hands are the hands of holy men. Our prayers will only have power with God if we are holy men. Linked with holy men in prayer are holy women, and they should adorn themselves modestly, not using gold or pearls or costly raiment. These things are loved by women of the world, but godly women will lay them aside. It is also the fashion among worldly women to have short hair, but godly women will have long hair, for this is according to the word of the Lord (1 Cor.11:15), and holiness is related to the word.

If we wish to live saintly lives then we must be willing for the Lord to search and try our hearts, and to reveal to us the flaws and faults that we cannot see ourselves. How easy it is for us to see the flaws in others, and how difficult it is to see our own! But if we are seeking after holiness, it is much more important for us to see our own faults than to see the faults of others. "Search me, O God, and know my heart: Try me, and know my thoughts: And see if there be any way of wickedness in me, and lead me in the way everlasting" (Ps.139:23,24). This is necessary for us in the life of holiness; the life that has power.

Holy living will mean that we must be right, both with God and with men. Where there is wrong, there must be confession of that wrong, and forgiveness sought. The apostle James says, "Confess therefore your sins (offences) one to another, and pray one for another" (5:16). We must he ready to confess our wrongs when we offend each other. This is essential in the life of holiness. If we sin against God in any matter, then we must be quick to confess our sin, and to seek forgiveness and cleansing by the blood of Jesus. When we have confessed it, then we must believe that He has forgiven it for His name's sake. The life of holiness will cost us something, but it will be worth it, for we shall have power with God and with men. Without sanctification, no man shall see the Lord (Heb.12:14).

This is seeing Him day by day, it is the daily experience of fellowship with Him. How vital then is holiness to the servant of Christ!

CHAPTER TEN: THE SECRET OF HOLY LIVING (ED NEELY)

A doubting disciple once asked a military general what he thought about the possibility of carrying out such commands as evangelizing the whole world, or living a holy life in the midst of a sinful and perverse generation. The general answered that the soldier or the bondservant never asks what is possible: he merely does his utmost to carry out his orders.

What Are Our Orders?

Peter, who had all too profound a knowledge of failure in the matter of holiness, was the apostle used to remind us of the commandment of the Lord (1): 'He who called you is holy, you also be holy in all your conduct, because it is written, "Be holy, for I am holy." Peter was quoting from Leviticus 11, a chapter describing rules of conduct for those who as a priesthood followed the LORD. The description found in this chapter nicely defines holiness: separation from the unclean, and separation to the pure. Can those who serve God in priestly capacity today seek anything less than separation from that which defiles and separation to the One who has made us pure?

The Christian believer is in a tug-of-war. Satan would separate us from godliness through sin. Christ would separate us from sin to godliness. There is nothing in us naturally that responds to the Lord; there is in each of us a sinful tendency that responds to Satan. Christ alone could say that Satan had nothing in Him. We reflect instead that which Paul felt most deeply: "O wretched man that I am! Who will deliver me from this body of death?" (2) Is it possible in view of our natures to live in the beauty of holiness? What are our orders?

The Secret of Holy Living

Paul tells the Romans (12:1) and us the secret of holy living: "I beseech you therefore, brethren, by the mercies of God, that you present your bodies a living sacrifice, holy, acceptable to God, which is your reasonable service." He also lets us know that attainment of holy living is a gradual thing demanding constant cleansing from the sinfulness that finds an answer in the 'old man' resident within us (3) and a pressing on to a growing, maturing holiness, a progressing practical sanctification, an increased Christlikeness: 'beloved, let us cleanse ourselves from all filthiness of the flesh and spirit, perfecting holiness in the fear of God" (4).

The Holy Spirit's Enabling

The Holy Spirit, so holy, so often grieved and even quenched, works with our spirits to enable us. He loves us and His constraint is the action of divine love. This progression of perfecting holy living is the kind of thing we see in the life of Peter and evidenced in the faithful serenity we observe in the elderly apostle John. Amid unspeakable trials, and given the most moving revelations, they remained serene and immovable. We can observe it also in the lives of godly saints around us, men and women whose experiences, both publicly in life and hidden with the Lord, have developed and are developing in them a quietness and confidence that can be a tremendous source of strength to us all.

They purvey for us in their daily walk the qualities of the fruit of the Spirit (5): 'love, joy, peace, longsuffering, kindness goodness, faithfulness, gentleness, self-control.' And in their imperturbability they generate quietude. Ancient Joshua gave a prescription and commitment that many readers will already have made personal: "As for me and my house, we will serve the LORD (6)".

Consciously Avoiding Sin

The avoidance of sin should be a very conscious activity in the life of every believer. A life of sanctity is necessitated by our calling: "Only let your conduct be worthy of the gospel of Christ" (7); "walk worthy of the calling with which you were called" (8). And it is prescribed by the future: "Therefore, since all these things will be dissolved, what manner of persons ought you to be in holy conduct and godliness" (9). It is called for because each believer is a temple of the Holy Spirit. It is the evidence of the thing into which we have been called, "a holy temple in the Lord, in whom you also are being built together for a dwelling place of God in the Spirit" (10). God Himself is "glorious in holiness" (11) and everything associated with Him is holy: His Spirit, His house and all in it, His priesthood, His nation, His calling, His Son. To all this we are also called, and to His holiness we must give practical expression. The Lord said He would never leave us nor forsake us (12).

A Recipe for Holy Living

Consider for a moment the holiness of the Son of God. Gabriel commented on it, demons testified to it, those who had seen His walk spoke to God about 'Your holy Servant Jesus.' He called Himself holy, addressing His Father as, "Holy Father ... We are one." This same One who walks with us, one with us, desires that that walk be a holy one. Paul rejoiced over believers in Rome: "But God be thanked that though you were slaves of sin, yet you obeyed from the heart that form of doctrine to which you were delivered. And having been set free from sin, you became slaves of righteousness" (13). "Slaves of righteousness" - that's the recipe for holy living.

Some Far-reaching Consequences

We don't live to ourselves. The extent of the holiness of my daily living reflects upon the witness of the gospel, the testimony of the saints among whom I live and worship, and upon men's reception of the Lord Himself. Even if my actions remain unobserved by those around who watch, lack of holiness undermines my communion with Christ and affects the spirit of unity with fellow-believers. The old hymn says: "Forgive the sins I now confess to Thee, Forgive the secret sins I cannot see." Constant confession and waiting upon the Lord are necessary tools for the development of holy living.

Building Upon One Another

Perhaps we too often forget or neglect the fact that other believers, fellow-strugglers against all the wiles of the devil, build upon our successes in overcoming the evil one. These little victories in our lives engender strength in others, just as evidence of commonly understood standards of purity and godliness in their lives encourage us in our fruitfulness. We build upon one another. We can also discourage our fellows by our behaviour, like the stone in a house, which displayed characteristics of a plague in Leviticus 14, if the infection were not corrected or the stone removed, the whole building would be infected. A little leaven can affect the whole lump.

If we are truly subject to the Lord and His commandments, if the love and care for each other that is enjoined upon us by the Lord is evident, all men will know that we are His disciples and that such discipleship is much to be desired. Christian believers who walk and work with us to a common end will be blessed. Those who did not know subjection and who lacked the love of God in the past caused other people instead to blaspheme (14). How sad if the lack of holiness in my walk should cause such disrespect to God in others!

Traps to Avoid

Of course, there are things to guard against in this matter of trying to live a holy life, traps to avoid. One of them is using a supposed standard of holiness as some sort of self-aggrandizing comparative issue. God took a very dim view of some in Israel who did so, deprecating their behaviour in Isaiah 65:3,5: "A people who provoke Me to anger continually to My face; ... Who say, 'Keep to yourself, do not come near me, for I am holier than you!'"

An exemplification of those words was uttered against such people all through Matthew 23. God does not much appreciate those with superior attitudes; folk who compare themselves with others with any kind of disdain in this matter of holiness are hypocrites because any such claim is unholy! Christ never ceased to be holy, yet He ate and drank with sinners; allowed a sinful woman to wash and anoint His feet; spent time with the raving maniac who further defiled himself by running naked amid the tombs. He came to seek and save the lost, and that could not be accomplished by shunning their company, then or now. We serve a God who cares, a Lord to whom all souls matter. Separation does not mean isolation. Like God, we must hate the sin and love the sinner, and we must beware of any hint of a 'holier than thou' attitude. Some have entertained angels unawares. We might wonder just in what form they appeared.

We return to that doubting disciple and his question: Is it possible ...? With God all things are possible!

(1) 1 Pet.1:15,16 (2) Rom.7:24 (3) 1 Jn.1:8,9 (4) 2 Cor.7:1 (5) Gal.5:22,23 (6) Josh.24:15 (7) Phil.1:27 (8) Eph.4:1 (9) 2 Pet.3:11 (10) Eph.2:21,22 (11) Ex.15:11 (12) Heb.13:5 (13) Rom.6:17,18 (14) Rom.2:24

CHAPTER ELEVEN: CALLED AS SAINTS (DAVID WOODS)

Once, when preoccupied with legitimate distractions in Paris' Charles De Gaulle airport, I didn't hear the boarding call for my flight home to Manchester. Right at the last moment I noticed the time, raced to the gate to be greeted by some disgruntled French ground staff. 'We've been calling for you. Please board immediately. You're the final passenger.' It had been a close call! God is calling too, but not all hear it. Some hear it, but don't respond as fully as God desires. It's a call to become an integral part of something that is so precious to Him - a call to be found among God's people: His saints who are gathered according to His will. Have you heard it and responded?

God's desire for every believer is that they be joined harmoniously with others and together obey the commands of the Lord and follow His teaching as it's been revealed in God's Word. Such believers will be baptised and added to a local church of God, and will enjoy meeting together for fellowship, for prayer, for teaching and for the Remembrance, or the 'Breaking of the Bread'. Such a group of disciples is known as a Church of God (1).

Paul greeted the individuals who together formed the local Churches of God in Rome and Corinth as those who were 'called as saints' and 'saints by calling' (2). Ananias, in his conversation with the Lord during the vision recorded in Acts 9, referred to the early Christians of the Church of God in

Jerusalem as 'Your saints' (3). Erroneous teaching has led many to follow a false tradition of recognising individuals of immense spiritual character as 'saints', who attain such a status only when their lives are reviewed by others after death. How far from the truth this is! God's Word reveals to us that those at Rome and Corinth were 'saints by calling.'

Looking at the original New Testament language brings us a proper sense of what the word 'saints' really means. The Greek foundation ('hagios') is a word that denotes something 'sacred' or 'holy', and is elsewhere simply translated as 'holy'. It's logical, then, to read 'saints' as 'holy ones'. When we place this alongside the wonderful scriptures of Ephesians 1 - 'He chose us in Him before the foundation of the world, that we would be holy and blameless before Him'(4) - we gain an altogether superior view of what 'saints by calling' conveys. It's not a designation based on an assessment made by man, but an eternal calling of God.

Of course, holiness is something that God desires from every believer. Our personal holiness facilitates a closeness of ongoing relationship with a holy God. As individuals, we are to be set apart to Him, and separate from the defilement of a corrupting world. When Paul wrote to the saints in Corinth he encouraged them with the words - let us cleanse ourselves from all defilement of flesh and spirit, perfecting holiness in the fear of God (5). Paul knew, all too well, the great struggle we have in maintaining personal holiness before our holy God. Defilement affects our 'flesh' and our 'spirit' and can lead to ruin. How right Paul was not to mention the 'soul' in that verse - our souls have been forever cleansed and made holy by the atoning work of Christ - it's in our bodies and minds before God that we're required to give effect to our salvation with fear and trembling (6).

We know those things that defile our flesh and spirit, but we're often guilty of continuing in them. How can we guard ourselves against such defilement? Some suggestions might be:

1) attempting to consciously live each moment appreciating the reality of the presence of God. If we know that the Holy Spirit indwells us and we seek to allow him to have His influence in all that we do, then our lives lived under such moment-by-moment direction will be holy lives.

2) laying hold of the wonderful promise of 1 John 1:9 – "If we confess our sins, He is faithful and righteous to forgive us our sins and to cleanse us from all unrighteousness". True and sincere confession and repentance before God removes the stains of sin. To confess to Him we must be speaking with Him - prayer is vital if we are to be holy people.

3) spending time in God's Word, reading His repeated calls for His people to be holy. This will show us the true standards by which we should live our lives - God clearly tells us what's expected! We're encouraged to 'consider Jesus' and to run 'fixing our eyes on Jesus' (7). He's the benchmark.

4) pre-worship self-assessment. The people of God have the great privilege of worshipping God in the Holy Place. From Psalm 24 we learn that only those with 'clean hands' and 'pure hearts' (cf. 'flesh and spirit') can ascend the hill of the Lord and stand in His holy place. The weekly practice of reviewing the

state of our lives in the knowledge that we will enter God's holy presence will have a profound impact on our lives.

"For this is the will of God, your sanctification ... that each of you know how to possess his own vessel in sanctification and honor ... God has not called us for the purpose of impurity, but in sanctification" (8). Vine tells us that 'sanctification is used of separation to God ... the separation of the believer from evil things and ways'(9). This is what we've been called to; this is the will of God! Holiness is something God desires of every believer, but His purposes don't stop there. He wants believers to enjoy what it means to be 'called as saints' - and so to live out lives of holiness alongside others. Look back at 1 Corinthians 1:2 and we'll notice that Paul reminds the saints that they are "those who have been sanctified in Christ Jesus, saints by calling".

It takes us back to the Old Testament time when God brought Israel out of Egyptian slavery. They were called out that they might be His holy people, a holy nation, a people who together would worship Him. He separated them from their past lives, gave them His commandments for holy living and constituted them as His holy nation when they accepted His covenant and were 'separated' to Him (10). This was all a shadow of what God does today with those released from the slavery of sin. He gives freedom so that we might, by subsequently obeying His laws and His commands, form His holy people. Read 1 Peter 2:4-10 again!

When Paul was writing his letters to the Church of God in Corinth he was dealing with some serious sins and unholy practices that were being accepted by the Church. At the outset, Paul reminded them that they were 'holy ones by calling.' It was only right that any blatant and tolerated sin was exposed and dealt with appropriately through discipline and ultimately excommunication of those caught up in the sin. The holiness of God's people had to be taken seriously. They had to learn what it meant to be sanctified in Christ Jesus. The same applies today. Those who are 'called as saints' have a personal, and collective responsibility, to demonstrate God's standard of holiness in a world that is so full of sin.

A good place to finish is Ephesians 1:18 – "I pray that the eyes of your heart may be enlightened, so that you will know what is the hope of His calling, what are the riches of the glory of His inheritance in the saints". God calls us to be 'saints'. Let's strive to be the holy ones He has called us to be.

Bible quotations from NASB: (1) see Acts 2:41-42, 1 Pet.2:4-5, Eph.2:19-22; 1 Cor.1:2 (2) Rom.1:7; 1 Cor.1:2 (3) Acts 9:13 (4) Eph.1:4 (5) 2 Cor.7:1 (6) Phil.2:12 (7) Heb.3:1; 12:2 (8) 1 Thess.4:3-7 (9) W.E. Vine, Vine's Complete Expository Dictionary of Old & New Testament Words (10) Deut.7:6; Lev.19:2; Ex.19:5

CHAPTER TWELVE: THE HOLINESS OF THE HOLY PLACE (JOHN TERRELL)

One of the most precious areas of teaching in the epistle to the Hebrews concerns the access of God's people, in priestly character, to the immediate presence of God in collective worship. Having dealt in previous chapters with the high priestly succession of our risen Lord, 'after the order of Melchezidek', the writer of the epistle reaches, in chapters 9 and 10, the climax of the matter as far as God's people are concerned. Here he deals with the entering in of our great High Priest into heaven itself, through His own blood (9:12), and finally in 10:19, with the access of the people of God in worship to that same sacred place.

Lest there be any confusion about the place described in 10:19 which we have boldness to enter by the blood of Jesus, it is helpful to begin at the beginning of chapter 9. There we have a description of the Tabernacle of the Old Covenant, with its two distinct compartments and their furnishings. This, we are told, was a 'sanctuary of this world'. Chapter 8 verses 1 and 2 has already referred in a general way to the place of service of our great High Priest today as the heavenly sanctuary, or "the true tabernacle which the Lord pitched, not man". That is where His wonderful present day ministry is, as we shall see.

We need to consider carefully, however, the early verses of chapter 9. In verses 6 and 7 we are reminded that the High

Priest of Israel had regularly entered 'the first tabernacle', called in verse 2, 'the Holy place'; but only once in the year on the Day of Atonement, entered the second tabernacle, called in verse 3, 'the Holy of holies'. At this point we need to note very carefully the words of verse 8, "the Holy Spirit this signifying, that the way into the holy place hath not yet been made manifest, while as the first tabernacle is yet standing". This is a critical point in the development of the teaching of Hebrews on the subject we are considering. Not so much because of the indication that a way once barred is now open, although that is true. But rather to note, for our present purposes, that now the expression 'the holy place' is being used in a new sense and with a new meaning. It now refers to the very presence of God in heaven which the risen Lord has entered in priestly service. Close reading of verse 8 shows that 'the holy place' of verse 8 is equated to the second tabernacle, or Holy of holies, of verse 3 and verse 7.

Exactly the same term, 'the holy place' is now employed throughout the remainder of the teaching of this passage of Hebrews 9 and 10. In verse 12 of chapter 9 this, 'the holy place', is where the Lord has entered once for all through His own blood, certainly corresponding to the place which the priests of Israel could only enter annually bearing the blood of atonement - the Holy of holies, the immediate presence of God. In verse 24 it is the place in heaven on which the earthly sanctuary of old was patterned; and is 'before the face of God', again describing the immediate divine presence only found in the Holy of holies of the Old Covenant. Verse 25 further clarifies this point by contrasting Christ's once-for-all qualifying sacrifice, with the year-by-year blood shedding of the Day of Atonement.

Then, finally, we have 'the holy place' in chapter 10 verse 19, which the people of God are invited to enter with boldness 'by the blood of Jesus'. This is the same, and now the only, 'holy place' in God's view; His own immediate holy presence. Our access is through a veil which, unlike that separating the holy and most holy places of the historical Tabernacle, is not a barrier but a way of access - 'His flesh'. We enter because of all that flows from the incarnation and the atoning death of God's Son at Calvary. It is the place of inestimable privilege where those forming the house of God and the holy priesthood, meet in priestly service with the One who is "great priest over the house of God" (10:21).

There is no question of continuing the concept of varying degrees of access to God as seen in Israel in the court of the Tabernacle, the holy place, and the most holy place. The earlier part of Hebrews chapter 10 makes this clear. "By one offering He hath perfected for ever them that are sanctified" (10:14); that completeness, that sanctification, ushers us into the most holy presence of God as worshippers, where our great High Priest dwells - 'the holy place', above.

CHAPTER THIRTEEN: WORSHIPPING IN THE BEAUTY OF HOLINESS (T.W. FULLERTON)

"Worship the LORD in the beauty of holiness". These words are used in Psalms 29:2; 96:9, and elsewhere. In at least four of the occurrences the marginal reading is, "in holy array". This seems to refer to the garments worn by the priests and Levites when engaged in the service of the sanctuary. God gave Moses instructions - regarding the garments of the priests "for glory and for beauty" to be worn by Aaron and his sons when engaged in priestly service (Ex.28). (An exception to this, in the case of the high priest, is found in Lev.16). The Levites were to be attired in white linen garments. In his book, The Temple, Its Ministry and Service, at the time of Jesus Christ, Dr Edersheim writes, "If either a priest or the high priest officiated without wearing the full number of his vestments, his service would be invalid". In the "holy array" there was a beauty, attractive to the eye of God and man. The beauty of the Lord (their) God was upon them (see Ps.90:17).

In the Temple the service of praise went on day and night (1 Chron.9:33; Ps.134:1). Dr Edersheim, in a chapter, "At night in the Temple", states than an essential part of the night service was the watching by priests and Levites at appointed posts. It was the duty of the Levites to guard the gates to prevent, as far as possible, the unclean from entering the sacred precincts.

A total of 240 Levites and 50 priests were placed in twenty-four stations about the gates and the courts. The Captain of the Temple had the responsibility of making a nightly tour of inspection to see that none on duty was asleep. When he approached, the watchers had to arise and salute him in a certain manner. If any was found asleep, be was punished; one mode of punishment being the setting of his garments on fire; then the others would see that he had been asleep; they would see his shame. No one knew at what time the Captain of the Temple would appear for inspection.

Persons who had some knowledge of the Temple services would be acquainted with the imagery used in the book of Revelation. (Edersheim suggests that certain features of the apostle John's writings indicate that he belonged to a priestly family). Those who were gathered in the churches of God to whom the book of Revelation was sent would be aware that, in addition to being "a spiritual house, to be a holy priesthood, to offer up spiritual sacrifices" (1 Pet.2:5), they were also on temple guard. The warning, "Behold, I come as a thief. Blessed is he that watcheth and keepeth his garments, lest he walk naked and they see his shame" (Rev.16:15), would convey the meaning of something corresponding to the burning of the garments of a guard found asleep by the Captain of the Temple.

The expressions, "in the beauty of holiness", "in holy array" and "let the beauty of the LORD our God be upon us" have an application to the people of God today. The righteousness of God through Jesus Christ is upon all them that believe. This righteousness is something that can never be damaged or marred in any way. We shall be eternally in the home He is preparing for us on the ground of this righteousness alone. But if the beauty of the Lord is to be upon us now, we must "follow after righteousness. In Revelation 19:8, we read of fine linen, white and pure, which is the righteous acts of the saints.

We are not suggesting that under the New Covenant "in holy array" has to do with our literal garments; neither do we, on the other hand, conclude that it is immaterial what garments the saints composing the holy priesthood should wear. The Scriptures are emphatic that we should be attired modestly and properly (1 Tim.2:9,10). We are professedly appearing before the Majesty on high and this, in itself, should guide us in the matter. We do, however, get some light on the spiritual and moral qualifications with which a holy priesthood should be arrayed. In Psalm 15 the question is asked, "LORD, who shall sojourn in Thy tabernacle? Who shall dwell in Thy holy hill?" In the answer to these questions we find some very searching conditions, both positive and negative.

One only has fulfilled these conditions perfectly. In Him was seen "the beauty of the LORD" in its fulness. As Great High Priest He ministers in the heavenly sanctuary on behalf of His people in the "holy array" of perfect righteousness. Nevertheless here, we suggest, is the standard of character, behaviour and speech to which a holy priesthood should aspire. If, when we search our hearts in the light of these requirements, we are conscious of failure, we should make haste through confession to seek the assurance of forgiveness and cleansing (1 Jn.1:9) lest our priestly service be in vain.

Let us consider briefly the various conditions laid down in Psalm 15. "He that walketh uprightly, and worketh righteousness". When walking uprightly a person is not afraid to be seen, there is no hiding out of sight, no walking in the darkness. The working of righteousness consists in the doing of the will of God consistently and continuously.

"And speaketh truth in his heart". The words of the lips and the intents of the heart should be in unison. With the ungodly are often found "fervent lips and a wicked heart". The words of Isaiah, used by the Lord to the Pharisees and scribes, "This people honoureth Me with their lips; but their heart is far from Me", were a sad commentary on Israel's spiritual condition. Their worship was vain worship; it was not "in truth".

"He that slandereth not with his tongue". A slanderer is a false accuser; one who spreads a false report about another with the object of damaging his character. "He that uttereth a slander is a fool", wrote Solomon. (Prov.10:18).

"Nor doeth evil to his friend, nor taketh up a reproach against his neighbour". The godly person is "a friend that loveth at all times". The word reproach has various meanings. Here it is referring to a report derogatory to the character or reputation of another. It may, or may not, be true. The love of God shed abroad in our hearts would teach us not to repeat it unless there is some vital reason for doing so; and not to spread it abroad. Such things are not to be indulged in as idle gossip.

"In whose eyes a reprobate is despised; but he honoureth them that fear the LORD". A reprobate is one whose moral sense is perverted. He is unable to stand in the day of testing but turns from the Lord and from His truth. In marked contrast, those who fear the Lord will cleave unto Him. In spite of human weaknesses the general trend of their lives will reveal a settled purpose. We should honour such. Sometimes we may be inclined to give undue prominence to those who have wealth and other qualifications. We should have the discernment to give honour to those whom God honours. He honours those that fear Him.

"He that sweareth to his own hurt, and changeth not". Here is one of the principles of godly behaviour, the lack of which has caused untold damage between men and nations. In Romans 1:31, "covenant-breakers" are classified among the lawless and ungodly. In many cases promises between individuals, and treaties or agreements between nations, are made with no intention of honouring them. In others, solemn covenants are broken because circumstances arise which make it disadvantageous to honour them. An example of this occurred in 1914 when a solemn agreement with a neighbouring nation was treated as "a scrap of paper". In their dealings with each other, and with their fellow-men, Christians should recognize the solemnity of making a promise or entering into an agreement. Much reproach had been incurred and many have been stumbled by failure in this matter. We should therefore ponder well the implications of a promise or an agreement before making them, and we should always fulfil them, even if it turns to our disadvantage.

"He that putteth not out his money to usury, nor taketh reward against the innocent". While the condemnation of usury primarily has an application to Israel (Deut.23:19,20), can it not be applied more widely to the practice of demanding exhorbitant rates of interest? Judas is a solemn example of one who took a reward against the innocent. There are other cases of this shameful practice on record in the Scriptures.

Here, then, in Psalm 15, we suggest, are the positives and negatives to be applied to the conduct of those who would appear before God as a holy priesthood "in holy array" or "in the beauty of holiness". May it not be that much of the lack of divine power among us is due to our failure here? Let us not presume to engage in priestly service unless our spiritual and moral condition is right before God, "For our God is a consuming fire" (Heb.12:29).

CHAPTER FOURTEEN: LIVING UNTO RIGHTEOUSNESS (J.H. JOHNSON)

"For hereunto were ye called: because Christ also suffered for you, leaving you an example that ye should follow His steps: who did no sin, neither was guile found in His mouth: who, when He was reviled, reviled not again; when He suffered, threatened not; but committed Himself to Him that judgeth righteously: who His own self bare our sins in His body upon the tree, that we, having died unto sins, might live unto righteousness" (1 Pet.2:21-24).

Through faith, Christ is our righteousness. The joy of this realization caused Murray McCheyne to write:

"Jehovah Tsidkenu, my treasure and boast;

Jehovah Tsidkenu! I cannot be lost!

By Thee I shall conquer, by flood and by field,

My cable and anchor, my breastplate and shield."

We rejoice in what Christ has done for us: in what He is for us. But now we have to live for Him. We have been saved to serve. We have been bought with a price and now we are to glorify God in our bodies, or as the hymn writer put it:

"Just as I am, young, strong and free,

To be the best that I can be

For truth and righteousness and Thee,

Lord of my life. I come."

Righteousness and Faith

Life for God begins by faith: (Rom.1:17), and life for God continues by faith; "My righteous one shall live by faith: and if he shrink back, My soul shall have no pleasure in him" (Heb.10:38). In Romans 3:20-22 faith and works of self-righteousness are contrasted. But in James, faith and works of faith (works which are the product of faith) go together: "What doth it profit, my brethren, if a man say he hath faith, but not works? can that faith save him? (Jas.2:14). Obviously the answer is "No!" If a man truly believes in Christ there will be some evidence, or ought to be, in his life. Even the repentant thief showed his faith by the words that he spoke to his fellow robber and then to the Lord Jesus. What he said was a work of faith.

Christ our Example

The negatives in our opening scripture (1 Pet.2:21-24) are very important. We are to cease from sin. We have been redeemed from our vain manner of life handed down from our fathers. The old sinful habits are to go. There was no guile in His mouth and there is to be none in ours. We are to speak the truth everyone with his neighbour. "Let your speech be always with grace, seasoned with salt", the salt of truth. If we are reviled, if hurtful derogatory remarks are made about us and to us let us remember the Lord - and not answer back in the same vein. Sometimes the cutting remarks come from those who should know better! If we suffer physically or mentally we must not threaten to get our own back, but commit ourselves to God, the Righteous Judge.

These words are easily said, but for some of us they are very hard lessons to learn. There is one occasion each week which is of great help to each of us - the Breaking of the Bread. On that occasion we meet together to bring to remembrance the holy, righteous, gracious life of our Lord Jesus given in death for us. In appreciative thankfulness we worship, praise and thank the God and Father of our Lord Jesus Christ, whose heart of mercy has been revealed by Him to us.

The psalmist says that men become like the objects of their worship (Ps.115:8). How important, then, that we have the right thoughts about God, about the God whom we worship, and especially about the Lord Jesus. On those occasions when Israel appeared before God to worship Him, there probably came the time when Aaron the High Priest, carried out the instruction given in Numbers 6:22-27 and (as in Lev.9:22) lifted up his hands toward the people and blessed them from the altar of burnt offering. You remember the blessing: "The LORD bless thee, and keep thee: The LORD make His face to shine upon thee, and be gracious unto thee: The LORD lift up the light of His countenance upon thee, and give thee peace."

And you remember what the Lord said the result would be - "So shall they put My name upon the children of Israel; and I will bless them". Did it happen? Did He bless them? Of course it happened. Of course He blessed. And the godly Israelites went home with the name of Jehovah their God upon them, that is, with something of the character of Jehovah their God. They took on the likeness of the God they worshipped.

Years ago I heard the late C.C. Beadsworth suggest the possibility that at the end of our time of worship on a Lord's day morning our Great High Priest, the Lord Jesus, turns towards us and with uplifted hands pronounces a similar blessing upon us. What a marvellous probability for those who worship in spirit and truth!

Righteousness and Goodness

In Romans 5:7 a distinction is made between a righteous man and a good man. "For scarcely for a righteous man will one die: for peradventure for the good man some one would even dare to die". In this context the righteous man is the man who does the right thing, who is scrupulously correct. He pays his debts, he doesn't pilfer his employer's goods, won't break the rules, even when it seems to others unimportant to observe them. This is the righteous man without grace (in this context).

The good man, on the other hand, is the person who is generous in his dealings with others, who, while recognizing the rights of others, does not always insist on his own rights, doesn't hold grudges. Christ was not righteous in the narrow sense of Romans 5:7. His righteousness included doing good and to His disciples He said: "Except your righteousness shall exceed the righteousness of the scribes and the Pharisees ye shall in no wise enter into the kingdom of Heaven" (Matt.5:20).

The righteousness of the scribes and the Pharisees was concerned with a rigid observance of the traditions of the elders which made void the word of God. It led to wrong interpretations of the Scriptures, for example, regarding the Sabbath, and of course to wrong thoughts about God - "with the perverse Thou wilt shew Thyself forward" (Ps.18:26). Those who twist the Scriptures will get twisted thoughts about God. And wrong thoughts about God and hardness of heart go together, as seen in the story of the man with the withered hand (Mk.3). The Lord "looked round about on them with anger, being grieved at the hardening of their heart". Hard hearts led them to take counsel together how they might destroy Him. Hard hearts led them to contemplate and plot the murder of the Son of God.

Hard hearts! Something to which all of us are so prone. Something to be on our guard against - that by the grace of God we shall not become hard-hearted because of what others say or do to us, and more importantly, that we shall not be the cause of someone else becoming hard in heart. The effect can be the life-long destruction of spiritual joy. "Today if ye shall hear His voice, harden not your hearts" is spoken to us, believers in the Lord Jesus Christ. Should it happen, let us take it to the Lord in prayer, ask for forgiveness for feeling hard. Ask for cleansing by the blood of Jesus. Ask for grace to think right and gracious thoughts towards the one whose remarks or attitude were unchristian.

The righteousness of the scribes and Pharisees was in the nature of a publicity campaign. "See how righteous I am - I pray, I fast, I give etc." It is a righteousness performed before men, a righteousness which produced feelings of pride and envy - hateful things in the sight of God. Our righteousness must exceed that. How moderate the language of the Lord! Avoid excessive, extravagant language. Say "Yes" and keep your word. Say "No" and mean it. We do our righteousness in secret and God sees and He rewards.

The Righteousness of Christ

The righteousness of Christ is something glorious. It is like Joseph's fruitful bough which goes over the wall. It reaches out and does good. It blesses. It brings joy and gladness to God and to men. "Greater joy have I none than this, to hear of my children walking in the truth" says John (3 Jn.v.7).

The Lord went about doing good. He stretched out His hand and touched the man full of leprosy and healed him. He stopped the funeral procession and gave the young man back to his mother because he had compassion on her. He healed a demon-possessed boy and gave him back to his father. He cast out a legion of demons from a demented man who lived among the tombs and restored him to his right mind. He stood still on the way to Jerusalem and the cross, stood still at the cry for mercy from a blind man and restored his sight. Stood still at a cry for mercy, for He could not go on, for He delights in mercy. On the cross He prays, "Father forgive them; for they know not what they do" and to the reviling, abusive, but now repentant thief, He says, "Today shalt thou be with Me in Paradise" (Lk.23:43).

We follow a Man who was righteous and who hated iniquity, hated sin and evil doing, but whose righteousness included doing good, being compassionate, showing mercy. By the grace of God, and only by His grace, and with the help of the Spirit of grace we follow His steps. He has left us an Example. On the night before the cross He took a towel and a basin and washed the disciples' feet. "I have given you an example", He said. How much we need to learn this lesson in humility; being prepared to do the menial tasks, the jobs nobody else wants to do.

Goodness, compassion, mercy, humility, being tenderhearted - there is so much in the righteousness of Christ. So much in living for righteousness. So much to rejoice our hearts.

Holiness and Righteousness

Of great importance in our living for righteousness is holiness - indeed without holiness there can be no righteousness. The Lord Jesus was the "Holy and Righteous One". Holiness and righteousness go together. Holiness is the inward state. Righteousness is the life lived, the deeds done consistent with the inward holy character. The world despises holiness, caricatures holiness. To the world holiness is a negation of pleasure, an austere, joyless way of life. The Christians know better. Holiness is first of all purity, cleanness, beauty. "Worship the Lord in the beauty of holiness" for the Lord is holy. He says "Be ye holy; for I am holy". Those passages in Revelation where John describes the throne of God and the holy city, new Jerusalem, bring to our hearts and minds something of the awesome beauty of God:

"And there were seven lamps of fire burning before the throne, which are the seven Spirits of God; and before the throne, as it were a glassy sea like unto crystal" (Rev.4:5,6) and; "the holy city of Jerusalem, coming down out of heaven from God, having the glory of God; her light was like unto a stone most precious, as it were a jasper stone, clear as crystal ... and the city was pure gold, like unto pure glass." (Rev.21:10,11,18).

The Lord was in daily communion with God His Father, daily in the presence of God in prayer. He is our example. By means of daily prayer we begin to take on His likeness. You remember Moses, how his face shone because he had been speaking to God. We may not be aware of it, but there is some effect on our spirits, some likeness to the One to whom we pray, produced in us.

Holiness and Joy

With holiness is joy. David knew this, and in Psalm 16 he wrote, "In Thy presence is fulness of joy". Those mighty beings in the immediate presence of God experience that fulness of joy as they cry continually, "Holy, holy, holy, is the Lord God, the Almighty, which was, which is and which is to come". We, too, can only know that joy as we are holy. There is no true joy apart from holiness. Paul overflowed with joy in all his affliction and those to whom Peter wrote rejoiced "with joy unspeakable and full of glory". To know joy like that we shall have to be holy, "to cleanse ourselves from all defilement of flesh and spirit, perfecting holiness in the fear of God" (2 Cor.7:1).

Our love for the Lord is surely greater now than on the day we first put our trust in Him. We have come to know more about Him. We have experienced His help and His presence in our lives, and we love the Lord more today than on the first day. Holiness and righteousness are also progressive as we see from Revelation 22:1: "He that is unrighteous, let him do unrighteousness still: and he that is filthy, let him be made filthy still: and he that is righteous, let him do righteousness still: and he that is holy, let him be made holy still" (Rev.22:11).

Men who take the downward path "proceed further in ungodliness" and those who respond to the "upward calling of God" make progress in holiness and righteousness. It is a law, a principle. It is like overcoming temptation, every time you overcome you become stronger to overcome the next temptation. So too in following Christ every time we confess Christ before men we become stronger. A great strengthening of Christian character takes place each time we confess Christ. It is like that great saying of Jephthah, "I have opened my mouth unto the LORD, and I cannot go back" (Judg.11:35). You know that people expect you to live up to what you have said and you are conscious that your confession makes you responsible before the Lord to be faithful to it (by His help).

Righteousness and Faith

We begin by faith and we continue by faith. We have no doubt at all that "the faith which was once for all delivered unto the saints", namely the teaching of the apostles for the disciples of the Lord Jesus, applies to ourselves and that we are responsible to be obedient to that teaching. But how can we be sure of the Lord's will for us in special circumstances, at particular times of crisis in our lives, or when we are deeply exercised about some problem?

Sometimes the Holy Spirit brings forcibly to our minds and hearts a word from the Scriptures or gives us a strong persuasion and we are assured of the way we should go, the course we should take, or that the Lord is with us in the trial. This is a personal experience. James 5:16-18 is relevant. Elijah was a righteous man who prayed according to the will of God because he was a man who was daily in the presence of God (1 Kin.17:1). Today the righteous are still men and women of faith who stand in the presence, pray in the Spirit and then "conclude" what the Lord's will is for them as in Acts 16:10. "Morning by morning" (Is.50:4) He has left us an example.

CHAPTER FIFTEEN: YOUR MOST HOLY FAITH (GEORGE PRASHER)

The faith which was once for all delivered unto the saints is also referred to by Jude as "Your most holy faith" (see verses 8, 20). Though not delivered all at once it has been delivered once for all, that is to say, there will be no new revelation of the will of God, since the Holy Scriptures are now complete. As the law of Moses was the essence of all the teaching in the Psalms and Prophets, and at the close of the Old Testament the LORD said "Remember ye the law of Moses My servant, which I commanded unto him in Horeb for all Israel, even statutes and judgements" (Mal.4:4), so the "things that Jesus began both to do and to teach" (Acts 1:1) have in essence what is contained in the epistles and these with the Gospels complete the canon of inspiration and contain the faith once for all delivered unto the saints.

The faith then was set forth by the Lord Jesus; the law and the prophets were until John It makes an interesting contrast the manner in which the law was given and that which the faith came the faith of our Lord Jesus Christ The law had its association with the mighty thunderings at Horeb, and the voice from heaven concerning which Israel requested that no word more should be spoken to them for they could not endure that which was enjoined" but the manner in which the faith came through the Lord Jesus had no such terrifying association. When He began to teach it is recorded that "All bare Him witness, and wondered at the words of grace which proceeded out of His mouth" (Lk.4:22)

Gently and tenderly as men were able to hear and receive came the doctrine of the Lord. His speech was indeed refreshing like the dew, and His doctrine such as would penetrate the hearts and consciences of the hearers. The Holy Spirit, too, followed up the good work commenced by the Lord and brought to the remembrance of the apostles what He had said He also showed things to come. It was through this inspiration of the Holy Spirit that the Gospels and the Epistles were written.

While, generally speaking, the faith includes the entire revelation conveyed through the New Testament i.e. the truth concerning salvation from the penalty of sin through faith in the finished work of Christ, together with the will of God for the daily guidance of His redeemed and gathered together people it should be noted that it is also spoken of as something distinguishable from our common salvation. Jude says: "Beloved while I was giving all diligence to write unto you of our common salvation I was constrained to write unto you exhorting you to contend earnestly for the faith which was once for all delivered unto the saints" (verse 3).

Here it is apparent that "our common salvation" has reference to what we have termed above salvation from the penalty of sin. This is the common portion of every' true believer in the Lord Jesus Christ. A salvation not common as to quality, but common only in the sense that each one who trusts the Saviour has the blessing m common and-what a blessing it is! eternal life, eternal sanctification and eternal glory. But there is more than all this. There is something that has its bearing upon present and progressive sanctification, upon doing those what things that are pleasing to the Lord upon the earth. This is what Jude refers to as the faith.

One outstanding feature of the faith is, that it can be held or kept only by a separate and gathered together people: the early churches of God in apostolic times being the ensample for the remaining part of the age. Individuals as such cannot keep the faith, nor can it find expression in sectarianism rather it is denied therein. Baptism in water in obedience to the Lord is an integral part of the faith, and yet in how many places this is rejected. The same is true of the remembrance of the Lord in the breaking of the bread. These ordinances of the Lord require that the disciple should find himself in association with others whose hearts have been reached and softened by the distilled dew of divine speech, and whose beings have been saturated by the showers of divine doctrine. Thus together we may grow till we "attain unto the unity of the faith, and of the knowledge of the Son of God, unto a full grown man, unto the measure of the stature of the fulness of Christ."

The faith then, is something in which we may be weak (Rom.14:1), or strengthened (Acts 16:5). The mind of the Lord, as conveyed by Paul, Silas and Timothy, resulted in the churches being strengthened in the faith, and Timothy is reminded how he could be a good minister of Christ Jesus, nourished in the words of the faith, and of the good doctrine which he had followed. We may turn aside from it, or we may continue in it (Acts 13:8;14:22): we may be obedient to the faith

(Acts 6:7), or we may deny the faith (1 Tim.5:8). There is sad and solemn possibility of making shipwreck concerning the faith. To avoid this it is ever needful for us to give due heed to the words of divine warning which will guide us past the shoals of men's opinions, and the rocks of unbelief.

The range and scope of the faith is very large. It has been well said that "the Person and work of Christ is the central truth of the faith, but, within its circumference are truths many and varied, embracing every responsibility both individual and collective. The doctrines of the faith reach up to the divine heights, of the Deity and atonement of Christ, and come down even to matters of temporal support, as in 1 Timothy 5:8. This passage reads: "But if any provideth not for his own, and specially his own household, he hath denied the faith, and is worse than an unbeliever."

The faith once for all delivered unto the saints, like the law in the past dispensation, gives instruction to regulate the lives of God's people in every phase of life, and incorporates in the main the moral law of the LORD. The duties of parents to children, and children to parents: responsibilities of masters towards servants, and servants towards masters: the believer's attitude towards the powers that be, and his rendering unto Caesar the things that are Caesar's: his position generally towards all men as to walking humbly and living soberly righteously and godly: his life in the assembly of God both toward God and the brethren every relationship in life is provided for in the faith once for all delivered unto the saints. If we want to live well pleasing to God in the home in the House of God, and in the world we must necessarily keep constant contact with the

Book, the Holy Writings, every word of which is given by inspiration of God and is profitable for doctrine, for reproof, for correction, for instruction which is in righteousness that the man of God may be perfect, throughly furnished unto all good works (2 Tim.3:16,17)

Probably among many of the children of God the principal departure from the faith is in matters pertaining to everyday living. Maybe today more than ever there is need for the clarion call to believers to give heed to what might be termed the small items of the faith which will curb the activities of the little foxes that spoil the vineyards Not infrequently the vineyards beautiful with blossom are spoiled by these destructive creatures We may be wonderfully clear on the great truths of the Deity of the Christ the value of His atoning death and His triumphant resurrection but if these great central truths fail to captivate the heart for the One who died and fill us with the constraining love of Christ that will force us to seek and do His will in the smaller details of life, we may become the barren vines that disappoint the owner, and are fit only for the burning.

Let us listen carefully to Jude's exhortation "But ye, beloved building up yourselves on your most holy faith praying in the Holy Spirit, keep yourselves in the love of God looking for the mercy of our Lord Jesus Christ unto eternal life" (verses 20, 21) Thus only may we escape the snares that would lead us to deny our only Master and Lord, Jesus Christ. Thus only will we at the close of the pathway be able to say, "I have kept the faith" (2 Tim.4:7).

CHAPTER SIXTEEN: HOLINESS THROUGH PROGRESSIVE SANCTIFICATION (HENDY TAYLOR)

Sanctification is a cardinal (of the greatest importance) truth of the gospel. It has an essential element of human responsibility in addition to the initial response of faith. Sanctification is that relationship with God into which men enter by faith in Christ, and is made possible through the death of Christ on the cross. 1 Corinthians 6:11 shows that the believer is immediately sanctified and the basis through which this is accomplished is the offering of the body of Jesus Christ once for all (Heb.10:10). The scriptural meaning of the word sanctification however is "prepared and set apart for holy uses". We are saved, therefore, for a purpose, and it is this which forms the subject of our consideration. It is often referred to as progressive sanctification.

It is important to recognize that the holy character referred to in 1 Thessalonians 3:13 is the result of this progressive sanctification, not that imputed to us when we believed in Christ. The latter set us apart in divine purpose with an object in view. Our objective is that the holy character of the individual is built up little by little as a result of obedience to the Word of God. This is God's will for the believer and His purpose in calling him by the gospel. He is to follow the example of Christ in the power of the Holy Spirit. From the time of creation when God blessed the seventh day and sanctified it (Gen.2:3), the unfolding of this fundamental divine principle can be seen. It is demonstrated by the call of Abraham to a separated life (Gen.12), the calling and separating of a nation for God's own possession (Ex.19), right through until the time when the Father sanctified the Son and sent Him into the world (Jn.10:36).

The Lord Jesus said, "I sanctify Myself" (Jn.17:19), and this culminated in the greatest sanctifying act of all when of deliberate choice He went to Golgotha to die. "Wherefore Jesus also, that He might sanctify the people through His own blood, suffered without the gate. Let us therefore go forth unto Him without the camp bearing His reproach" (Heb.13:12-13). How then can this purpose be achieved? First of all, it is through the word of God. The Lord's prayer in John 17 contains the words "sanctify them in the truth, Thy word is truth".

It is only as we are obedient and follow God's word that we can know the true blessedness of such an experience. The Holy Spirit is the Agent through whom the work of sanctification is accomplished. The apostle Paul knew the powerful experience of this work as demonstrated in Romans 15:13 and 1 Thessalonians 4:7-8. The Spirit's indwelling power, presence and divine unction will enable us increasingly to "follow after peace with all men, and the sanctification without which no man shall see the Lord" (Heb.12:14).

It is the will of God that our individual lives as believers should be free from moral defilement. His desire is to sanctify us so that as whole individuals we may be preserved entire without blame in spirit, soul and body (1 Thess.5:23). Through the sacrifice of Christ and the shedding of His precious blood, the members of our own body, which were once committed to the service of sin and uncleanness, are now to be devoted to the service of righteousness as they are set apart to do His will. "God called us not for uncleanness, but in sanctification" (1 Thess.4:7). It is a responsibility laid upon us all to quench and quell the fleshly lusts that war against the soul. Being sanctified has the effect of helping to form our whole moral standing before the Lord. Living in a world of declining moral standards and values, how important it is that we should answer to this call!

The solemn warning which Paul gives to the Thessalonians should be even more serious for us today when chastity, clean living and upright moral standards are the subject of questioning, mockery and even rejection. Enshrined in the truth of baptism is the need to appreciate the change that has taken place in our lives, that we no longer present our members unto sin as instruments of unrighteousness, but present ourselves unto God as alive from the dead, and our members as instruments of righteousness unto God (Rom.6:12-14). The consecration of Aaron and his sons as priests helps us to understand what is involved in this aspect of sanctification. There was the initial separation to divine service, but the continuing need for day-to-day sanctification still had to be met. The ear, the hand, the foot and the eyes are set apart for God, to do His will and to walk in His ways, listening to His word and walking in the path He has marked out for us, perfecting holiness in the fear of the Lord. How vital, therefore, that day by day we exhibit in our persons and lives the purity and holiness of character for which God has separated us to be to His glory and as a witness and testimony to those around us.

"I beseech you therefore, brethren, by the mercies of God, to present your bodies a living sacrifice, holy, acceptable to God, which is your reasonable service. And be not fashioned according to this world: but be ye transformed by the renewing of your mind, that ye may prove what is the good and acceptable and perfect will of God" (Rom.12:1-2).

As well as being set apart for holy living we are to be sanctified in truth. The Lord in His prayer before going to Calvary expressed the strong desire and burden of His heart that all those who were to be called saints might be one. Not only one in one Body, which is a glorious concept, but one in a positive visible unity that would be a witness in the world that those who saw it might believe and know that the Father has sent the Son (Jn.17:21-23). His will is that we should be united in service and testimony with others who share a common desire to be obedient to His will and subject to His Word and authority. The call of God comes to us to separate ecclesiastically.

The one who realizes he is in the place of unrighteousness and separates himself or out-purges from those who are walking contrary to the teaching of Scripture, is called "a vessel unto honour, sanctified, meet for the Master's use, prepared unto every good work" (2 Tim.2:21). The Lord Jesus Christ is in the outside place and He asks us to come out to Him. It is only by obedience to His word that we can know experimentally the fulness of being sanctified for His service.

In Leviticus 11:44, the Lord said to Israel, "I am the LORD your God: sanctify yourselves therefore, and be ye holy; for I am holy". His desire and purpose have not changed for us, for these words are repeated "it is written, Ye shall be holy; for I am holy" (1 Pet.1:15-16). God's purpose is that we should be a people together, a holy nation, separated to Him for His service both Godward in the matter of worship and manward in the matter of testimony in the Gospel. Have we responded to the call of God to separate, to withdraw from that which is contrary to revealed truth and to follow after righteousness and be found amongst His people in churches of God? Our relationship with Christ in the Church His Body brings an eternal state of perfect sanctification (Eph.5:25-27). Our relationship as a united people for God in this day and generation is conditional upon our obedience to His word and our behaviour in holding fast to the revealed truth of God. "... how men ought to behave themselves in the house of God, which is the church of the living God, the pillar and ground of the truth" (1 Tim.3:15).

To be a saint is not achieved by acts of exceptional holiness but simply as is described by the apostle in 2 Thessalonians 1:10 - "them that believed". But this is only the beginning. The saint is to follow sanctification. He must be obedient to the claims of God upon him both as an individual believer and in answering the call of God to separate in divine service with the people of God. "I will dwell in them, and walk in them; and I will be their God, and they shall be My people" (2 Cor.6:16). God grant us the desire to take heed to the exhortation of Peter which so beautifully epitomises our consideration: "Sanctify in your hearts Christ as Lord" (1 Pet.3:15).

CHAPTER SEVENTEEN: THE HOLY CHARACTER OF GOD'S KINGDOM (GEORGE PRASHER)

The moral character of the kingdom of God is clearly seen in the Old Testament Scriptures. Prior to the establishment of the kingdom in Israel God gave His law, an instrument for the government of the nation. This was the moral law, the statutes of which are found in Exodus 20, and the judgements in following chapters.

The moral law was basic in regard to the kingdom, and the willingness of the people to accept its obligations was required by the LORD before the covenant could be ratified and sealed by blood. See Exodus 19 and 24. "The law," we read, "is holy, and the commandment holy, and righteous, and good" (Rom.7:12). God designed that the holiness of the law should be displayed in His people. The holy law was given to a people to whom God said, "Ye shall ... be holy, for I am holy" (Lev.11:45). It was His standard, and where He governs He can set no standard of a lower character.

There was another aspect of law given to Israel - the ceremonial, which followed the moral aspect, and came after the establishment of the kingdom. It was of a different nature, and was secondary in importance, being only (with meats and drinks and diverse washings) carnal ordinances, imposed until a time of reformation (Heb.9:10).

It is sad that in Israel's history the lesser aspect of the law was often given a place of greater importance than it should have had, and the tradition of the elders even made void the word of God. This the Lord had occasion to expose when the Pharisees and certain of the scribes complained that His disciples ate their bread with unwashed hands. He said: "Well did Isaiah prophesy of you hypocrites, as it is written, 'This people honoureth Me with their lips, but their heart is far from Me. But in vain do they worship Me, teaching as their doctrines the precepts of men. Ye leave the commandment of God, and hold fast the tradition of men. For Moses said, 'Honour thy father and thy mother; and, He that speaketh evil of father or mother, let him die the death': but ye say, 'if a man shall say to his father or his mother, 'That wherewith thou mightest have been profited by me is Corban', that is to say, Given to God; ye no longer suffer him to do aught for his father or his mother; making void the word of God by your tradition, which ye have delivered: and many such like things ye do" (Mk.7:6-18).

Then He went on to show how they made void God's word, and rejected the commandment of God. In these words He rebuked the Pharisees and the scribes, then He taught the multitudes, saying, "Hear Me all of you, and understand: There is nothing from without the man, that going into him can defile him: but the things which proceed out of the man are those that defile the man." To the disciples He explained, "Whatsoever from without goeth into the man, it cannot defile him because it goeth not into his heart, but into his belly, and goeth out into the draught. This He said, making all meats clean" (Mk.7:14-19).

Here we find all the force of the Lord's authority directed against exalting man's tradition to take the place of the moral law of God. We judge this is something to which we need to pay attention in our day. Who that has any measure of spiritual discernment can fail to see that in so many instances man's tradition has made void the law of God? Very largely today man's fear of God "is a commandment of men which hath been learned by rote" (Is.29:18, RV margin).

The moral law of God then had two sides, that which was Godward, and that which was manward, and it has been, with one exception, incorporated in the faith which was once for all delivered unto the saints. It regulates the conduct of the disciple towards God and man. We should guard against the error that the moral requirements of the law have no bearing on believers in this dispensation. So far as our salvation from hell is concerned the law has no place, since we are saved by grace, and not by works, but God expects "that the ordinance of the law might be fulfilled in us, who walk not after the flesh, but after the spirit" (Rom.8:4).

Let us place the ten words of the law over against the words of the faith, or apostles' teaching.

(1) "Thou shalt have none other gods before Me" (Ex.20:3). "Neither be ye idolaters." "Flee from idolatry" (1 Cor.10:7,14).

(2) "Thou shalt not make ... a graven image ... Thou shalt not bow down thyself unto them, nor serve them" (Ex.20:4,5). "My little children, guard yourselves from idols" (1 Jn:5.21).

(3) "Thou shalt not take the Name of the LORD thy God in vain (vanity or falsehood)" (Ex.20:7). Whilst Israel were commanded not to take the LORD's glorious and fearful name in vain, or for falsehood, the teaching of the New Testament is, "Swear not at all" (Matthew 5:84). See also James 5:12.

(4) "Remember the sabbath day to keep it holy" (Ex.20:8). The Lord did good deeds on the sabbath day, and we read, "Let no man ... judge you in respect of ... a sabbath day" (Col.2:16). The sabbath is one of many types. Of the ten commandments this is the only one which is excepted from the faith. Our Lord rose from the tomb on the first day of the week, and this day (not the sabbath) is marked as the day on which the disciples came together to break bread (Acts 20:7).

(5) "Honour thy father and thy mother: that thy days may be long upon the land which the Lord thy God giveth thee" (Ex.20:12). We have already seen the Lord's reference to this matter in Mark 7. Besides this we have Paul's words in Ephesians 6:1-8, "Children. obey your parents in the Lord: for this is right. Honour thy father and mother (which is the first commandment with promise), that it may be well with thee, and that thou mayest live long on the earth."

(6) "Thou shalt do no murder" (Ex.20:18). "Whosoever hateth his brother is a murderer: and ye know that no murderer hath eternal life abiding in him" (1 Jn.3:15). "He that loveth not abideth in death" (1 Jn.3:14).

(7) "Thou shalt not commit adultery" (Ex.20:14). Among those who shall not inherit the kingdom of God are "forni-

cators ... adulterers, nor effeminate, nor abusers of themselves with men" (1 Cor.6:9). "Let marriage be had in honour among all, and let the bed be undefiled: for fornicators and adulterers God will judge" (Heb.13:4). Says the Lord Jesus, "But I say unto you, that every one that looketh on a woman to lust after her hath committed adultery with her already in his heart" (Matt.5:28).

(8) "Thou shalt not steal" (Ex.20:15). Let him that stole steal no more: but rather let him labour, working with his hands the thing that is good, that he may have whereof to give to him that hath need" (Eph.4:28). This person will find it more blessed to give than to steal.

(9) "Thou shalt not bear false witness against thy neighbour" (Ex.20:16). But speaking truth in love, may grow up in all things unto Him, which is the Head. Wherefore, putting away falsehood, speak ye truth each one with his neighbour: for we are members one of another" (Eph.4:15,25).

(10) "Thou shalt not covet anything that is thy neighbour's" (Ex.20:17). "Take heed, and keep yourselves from all covetousness for a man's life consisteth not in the abundance of the things which he possesseth (Lk.12:15). See also 1 Timothy 6:6-10.

When the Lord was asked by a lawyer, "Master, which is the great commandment in the law?" He said to him, "Thou shalt love the Lord thy God with all thy heart, and with all thy soul, and with all thy mind. This is the great and first commandment. And a second like unto it is this, Thou shalt love thy neighbour as thyself. On these two commandments hangeth the whole law, and the prophets (Matt.22:35-40).

This is further emphasized in the words of Paul in Romans 13:9,10, "Thou shalt not commit adultery, Thou shalt not kill, Thou shalt not steal, Thou shalt not covet, and if there be any other commandment, it is summed up in this word, namely, Thou shalt love thy neighbour as thyself. Love worketh no ill to his neighbour: love therefore is the fulfilment of the law." This throws into relief the saying of the Lord in John 14:15, "If ye love Me, ye will keep My commandments." This is that love that never faileth.

"Love suffereth long, and is kind; ... envieth not ...vflaunteth not itself, is not puffed up, doth not behave itself unseemly, seeketh not its own, is not provoked, taketh not account of evil rejoiceth not in unrighteousness, but rejoiceth with the truth ... beareth all things, believeth all things, hopeth all things, endureth all things. Love never faileth" (1 Cor.13:4-8).

"If ye fulfil the royal law, according to the Scripture," says James, "Thou shalt love thy neighbour as thyself, ye do well." Then he goes on to say, "So speak ye, and so do, as men that are to be judged by a law of liberty" (2:8,12); and in James 1:25 he terms this law of liberty 'the perfect law'. It is this that is prominent when we consider the moral character of the kingdom of God. The "thou shalt-nots" are present, but not with the same emphasis, because against the fruit of the Spirit "there is no law". "And they that are of Christ Jesus have crucified the flesh with the passions and the lusts thereof" (Gal.5:23, 24).

One little girl wanted another to join in doing something wrong, but the latter objected because, said she, "Father would not like me to do that." "But father would not know," rejoined the first girl. The knowledge of her father's will, however, was sufficient to cause this little person to abstain from what she knew he would not allow, though she had no commandment from him as to this particular act. Here is the law of love in operation. There is a story told of a gentleman who took his collie to the city. For a while, each time he went out, the lead was attached to the neck of the dog. Then one day as Jock held up his head to have the lead put on his master said, "No Jock, you are to have your liberty today". When on the street the dog darted off in great excitement and the owner wondered, as he bounded out of sight, Will I ever see him again? Very soon, however, Jock reappeared and bounced towards his master's side. He was bound by a lead that was stronger than leather - the perfect law of liberty. He loved his master.

"The kingdom of God is not eating and drinking, but righteousness, peace, and joy in the Holy Spirit" (Rom.14:17). The moral character of the kingdom has righteousness to the front. In some kingdoms, "Does it pay"? or, "Is it good policy"? is first and foremost, and whether or not it is right does not weigh heavily. But "the unrighteous shall not inherit the kingdom of God" (1 Cor.6:9). We should be seekers of His kingdom, and His righteousness, for they must go together. Pious expressions and use of the title, Lord, Lord, is no warrant either for entrance into or assurance that one is in the kingdom. What can be more solemn and sad than the fact that many engage in prophecy, and doing mighty works by the name of Christ, and yet in the coming day He will protest saying, "I never knew you: depart from Me, ye that work iniquity"? Then the Lord says, "Every one therefore which heareth these words of Mine, and doeth them, shall be likened unto a wise man, which built his house upon the rock: and the rain descended, and the floods came, and the winds blew, and beat upon that house; and it fell not: for it was founded upon the rock" (Matt.7:22-25).

"He that herein serveth Christ is well-pleasing to God, and approved of men. So then let us follow after things which make for peace, and the things whereby we may edify one another" (Rom.14:18,19). But in writing on the moral character of the kingdom we are reminded of the immoral world in which we live. Perhaps as never before in the world's history violence and sexual vice prevail. Those who desire to bear the character of the kingdom need to have deep exercise of heart before God to the end that the word of Christ may dwell richly within. This will be necessary if we are to escape the corruption that is in the world by lust (2 Pet.1:4).

"Be not ye partakers with them," says Paul to the Ephesians, "for ye were once darkness, but are now light in the Lord: walk as children of the light (for the fruit of the light is in all goodness and righteousness and truth), proving what is well-pleasing unto the Lord; and have no fellowship with the unfruitful works of darkness, but rather even reprove them ; for the things that are done by them in secret it is a shame even to speak of" (Eph.5:7-12). We would indeed be ashamed to speak of these things, but in the holy Scriptures these matters are dealt with in Spirit-restrained terms, and we can use the words of the Spirit to draw the attention of believers, especially young believers, to the need for us to be like Joseph who fled in the hour of temptation.

"Flee fornication" (1 Cor.6.18), is Paul's injunction to the saints. All forms of uncleanness should be eschewed by the disciple of the Lord Jesus. "Keep thyself pure ('hagnog' pure, chaste, modest, innocent, blameless) (1 Tim.5:22), were the apostle's words to his child Timothy; and the Lord Jesus says, "Blessed are the pure ('katharoi', clean, pure, unsoiled) in heart: for they shall see God" (Matt.5.8). The city of Corinth is said to have been a cesspool of iniquity, and the gospel of God having reached men and women there, reached them in their condition as fornicators, idolaters, adulterers, effeminate and abusers of themselves with men, thieves, covetous, drunkards, revilers and extortioners, "but ye washed yourselves" (1 Cor.6:9-11, RV margin) was the testimony of Paul concerning those that had received the grace of God. As they had been sanctified eternally in Christ Jesus they then realized that their part was to wash themselves from the uncleanness of their former lives. This is the intention of the Holy Spirit.

"For the grace of God hath appeared, bringing salvation to all men, instructing us, to the intent that, denying ungodliness and worldly lusts, we should live soberly and righteously and godly in this present world; looking for the blessed hope and appearing of the glory of our great God and Saviour Jesus Christ; 'who gave Himself for us, that He might redeem us from all iniquity, and purify unto Himself a people for His own possession, zealous of good works" (Titus 2:11-14).

It is in the midst of this purified people that the kingdom of God can be found. This does not mean that the saints within the kingdom are always blameless, or that they do not often fail and commit sin. It is still true that "if we say that we have no sin, we deceive ourselves, and the truth is not in us", but there is divine provision for the failures of God's people in the blood of Jesus His Son which cleanseth us from all sin and unrighteousness. (1 Jn.1:8,9). In Psalm 144:12-15 there is a pen picture of those who form God's kingdom. We quote the verses because of their beauty: "When our sons shall be as plants grown up in their youth; And our daughters as corner stones hewn after the fashion of a palace; When our garners are full, affording all manner of store; And our sheep bring forth thousands and ten thousands in our fields; When our oxen are well ladan; When there is no breaking in, and no going forth, And no outcry in our streets: Happy is the people, that is in such a case: Yea, happy is the people, whose God is the LORD."

CHAPTER EIGHTEEN: THE NAZIRITE'S HOLY VOW (GEORGE PRASHER)

Separation to the LORD was the outstanding feature in a person who undertook the vow of the Nazirite (see Numbers 6). The Israelite nation were a separated people - they had been redeemed by blood in Egypt, and separated from Egypt by the waters of the Red Sea. A further sanctification to God as a holy nation was effected by the covenant of obedience with the blood of sprinkling, at the time of Exodus 19-24, when the LORD avouched Israel to be His people, and they avouched the LORD to be their God.

Within this separated nation appeared various circles were separation to God was more or less enjoined. The nation was the largest circle. Then the men of war are seen - men within certain ages, and of ability for war. The tribe of Levi was separated to special service in connection with God's dwelling, and were a smaller circle than the men of war. Then the smallest circle of all was the family of Aaron, separated to serve at the altar, and within God's house.

A thrice holy God had taken up His abode within the camp, and His laws, which are in keeping with His holiness, had to be recognised. There was a place for all, and each had to be in his place. While, however, such separation and holiness were characteristic of the nation, there was beyond all this a special separation unto the LORD which a man or a woman could undertake; it was an individual matter, an intensive separation, a special vow.

Certain men of power for God in their day were marked by the Nazirite vow. For instance the mighty Samson was to be a Nazirite from birth; his mother received instructions before he was conceived to act in harmony with this vow of separation. The child was to be a Nazirite unto God from the womb to the day of his death. Such a one the Spirit of God began to move in the camp of Dan (see Judges 13). It must always be so, the Holy Spirit finds room for movement in men separated unto God.

Which of us has not mourned over the story of Samson's later failures and trials? Yet all these are but solemn examples of the sorrow and loss which must ever attend failure in maintaining separation unto God. The young man of mighty strength, the destroyer of the Philistines ('wallowers in the dust'), the sustainer of injustice at the hands of the men of Judah, is soon in the valley of Sorek, which means 'tendril of the vine'; and at last is asleep on the knees of Delilah with the seven locks of his head shaven off. "I will go out as at other times, and shake myself," said he, "But he wist not that the LORD was departed from him" (Judg.16).

As Hannah poured out her soul before the LORD and pleaded for a man child to be granted unto her, part of her vow was "There shall no razor come upon his head." Here again is a sign of that special separation unto God. Remember how that boy came to know the LORD, and to serve Him in the power of the Spirit, which marks those "Separated unto the LORD."

Was it to be wondered at that in Samuel's days" all the house of Israel was drawn together after the LORD" (1 Sam.7:2).

Examples might be multiplied, but we desire instead to draw attention to some solemn teaching contained in the vow of the Nazirite:

1st. The Nazirite had to deny himself certain natural appetites: "He shall separate himself from wine and strong drink; he shall drink no vinegar of wine, or vinegar of strong drink, neither shall he drink any liquor of grapes, nor eat fresh grapes or dried. All the days of his separation shall he eat nothing that is made of the grape-vine, from the kernels even to the husk" (verses 3,4). "Wine that maketh glad the heart of man" (Ps.104:15) he was denied. Grapes fresh or dried with all their sweetness and food value he must turn away from. Here is self-denial in the matter of eating and drinking.

2nd. "All the days of his vow of separation there shall no razor come upon his head ... he shall let the locks of the hair of his head grow long" (verse 5); The Spirit of God says: "Doth not even nature itself teach you, that, if a man have long hair, it is a dishonour to him?" (1 Cor.11:14). It is therefore an honour or glory to the man to have short hair, but this glory he must deny himself while he is under the vow of the Nazirite. Here is self-denial in man's glory.

3rd. "He shall not come near to a dead body. He shall not make himself unclean for his father, or for his mother, for his brother, or for his sister, when they die: because his separation unto God is upon his head. All the days of his separation he is holy unto the LORD" (verses 6, 7). Here is self-denial in man's natural affections. His appetite, his glory, and his affections must be under divine control.

"The kingdom of God to-day is not eating and drinking, but righteousness and peace and joy in the Holy Spirit", yet these lessons in self-denial should speak loudly to us if we desire to know experimentally the power of God's Spirit within. The Master's words come to our mind: "If any man would come after Me, let him deny himself, and take up his cross daily, and follow Me" (Lk.9:28). Whatever we indulge in that hinders our spiritual progress should occasion us exercise and confession before God, that is, if we desire to know power with God. The great need of the hour is that of men separated and consecrated unto the LORD.

"The trivial round, the common task,

Will furnish all we need to ask;

Room to deny ourselves, a road

To bring us daily nearer God."

When the Nazirite had fulfilled the days of his vow of separation he offered to God a ewe-lamb for a sin offering, a he-lamb for a burnt offering, both of the first year, and a ram for a sacrifice of peace offering, besides the meal offering and the drink offering. This would be a solemn reminder that although he had fulfilled the days of his separation unto his God, still he owed his acceptance before God to the sacrifices which pointed to the Person and work of Christ. The most completely separated man is yet a sinner, and a victim must suffer and die for him. Indeed the greater the separation and consecration the more the fact of sin will be appreciated. How precious for such to revel in the efficacy of the sacrifice, the completeness of the acceptance before God, and the fulness of the fellowship with God! The believer to-day finds all these in Christ.

Though deeply conscious of unworthiness as he saw others die in his room and stead there is one very interesting feature in the concluding ceremony: "The Nazirite shall shave the head of his separation. at the door of the tent of meeting, and shall take the hair of the head of his separation, and shall put it on the fire which is under the sacrifice of peace offerings" (verse 18).

This is something unique in the law of the offerings. We recall no other instance when any part of man found a place on the copper altar of burnt offerings. Surely it speaks most loudly of the value to God of that head of separation, shadowing the coming perfect One, who though not a Nazirite. in the strict sense, was wholly devoted to God, and who would do all God's will. And how very precious to God is everyone today who devotes himself increasingly to separation in order that he may experience more of the power of God within! "But know that the LORD hath set apart him that is godly for Himself" (Ps.4:3).

"O Christ, Thou heavenly Lamb,

Joy of the Father's heart,

Now let Thy love my soul inflame;

Fresh pow'r to me impart."

CHAPTER NINETEEN: PRACTICAL SANCTIFICATION (JOE BENNISON)

Sanctification is both a finished act and a continuing process. Every believer is sanctified, set apart, in his relationship to God through the sacrificial work of Christ. The sinner plays no active part in this aspect of sanctification. He hears, believes, and rejoices in it through faith in Christ alone. This can never be repeated it is once for all. Such a one has been "sanctified through the offering of the body of Jesus Christ once for all" (Heb.10:10).

Though that is the privileged position of every born-again soul through the precious blood of Christ, there is the other aspect, that practical sanctification whereby we become vessels "unto honour sanctified, meet for the Master's use." I was very interested in the' experience of a dear friend who had recently accepted the Lord Jesus as his own Saviour. You will probably be amused, but my friend had been a heavy smoker: on the night of his decision he brushed his mouth out with common salt and thereafter bathed himself completely. To use his own words, he said "I was anxious in my new life to be clean inside and out." You ask, 'Is that essential'? and I would answer, 'no'! But does it not indicate a real desire to be well-pleasing to the Lord? Indeed my thoughts went immediately to David's exercise of heart when he cried, "Purge me with hyssop, and I shall be clean: wash me, and I shall be whiter than snow." Granted there is a spiritual significance, nevertheless it does indicate a desire to be clean inside as well as outside.

Sanctification then is used of the believer's daily life and walk. This can only be learned from God through His word. The Lord Jesus said, "Sanctify them in the truth, Thy word is truth" (Jn.17:17). The word of God will furnish us with all the help and guidance that we require. "Wherewithal shall a young man cleanse his way?" The simple answer is, "By taking heed to the word of God." It both cleanses and keeps us clean. There is ever the danger of turning towards the old life, unless we are constantly following after holiness in the power of the Holy Spirit. What a dishonour to go back to the beggarly elements of the world! Paul wrote of Demas having forsaken him, having loved this present world.

God has a purpose for each of us and our members are the instruments with which He has provided us for the accomplishing of this. He says emphatically, "Ye are not your own, ye were bought with a price"; or, to quote another verse from 1 Corinthians 6, "The body is not for fornication, but for the Lord; and the Lord for the body." One would naturally hesitate to use such an ugly word, apart from the fact that it is in the inspired writings, but having quoted it I do wish to be straight on this solemn subject. Here is the truth that one has been endeavouring to present. "The body is not for fornication, but for the Lord." It is the sanctuary of the Holy Spirit, in which we are to glorify God.

You may be shocked and possibly offended that I should mention such a matter. I know that it is a delicate matter and one certainly does not wish to hurt anyone's feelings, but we must remember that the Holy Spirit through Paul is raising a warning note. It may not be necessary to name such a matter to many of the Lord's dear children, but this evil had crept into the Church of God in Corinth. Some had already been caught in the snare of the evil one, having been drawn aside from the pursuit of holiness.

James in his forthright and practical manner tells us, when dealing with the subject of temptation, "Each man is tempted, when he is drawn away by his own lust." The devil appeals to the lusts of the flesh by the enticements of the world. The world, the flesh, and the devil operate together, and that means for every one of us constant conflict. The body is a good servant but a bad master. Paul wrote, "I keep under my body." In his letter to the Thessalonians, he clearly sets forth the use and the abuse of the body. "Finally then, brethren, we beseech and exhort you in the Lord Jesus, that, as ye received of us how ye ought to walk and to please God, ... that ye abound more and more. For ye know what charge we gave you through the Lord Jesus. For this is the will of God, even your sanctification, that ye abstain from fornication" (1 Thess.4:1-3). It is abundantly clear that we are to be holy in all manner of living. "Be ye holy; for I am holy," is the unchanging demand of our God.

Then our Lord left us an example, that we should follow His steps. He makes it clear beyond doubt that such a walk of holiness is possible. Listen to what He says: "Blessed are the pure in heart, for they shall see God." What an objective! What a possibility! To be like Him. "Like Thee in faith, in meekness, love, in every heavenly grace." Surely this should be the desire of every redeemed heart, a longing that we should be all that He would desire us to be! Our bodies are the temple of the Holy Spirit, moreover they are the Lord's and it is only right that they should be used for His glory; sanctified, meet for the Master's use.

In closing let me remind you of that veteran of spiritual conflict, Paul, scarred with the wounds of battle. He uses these significant words "Henceforth let no man trouble me: for I bear branded on my body the marks of Jesus." There is no doubt that he is referring to the actual brands which his poor, scarred body bore; marks inflicted by the enemies of the Lord, and evidences of his faithfulness. Ah, yes, but surely there is something deeper, and more indelible than the brands on his body; they are the marks of ownership, and proofs of possession. He belonged to that One of whom he said, "I am ready, not to be bound only, but also to die, ... for the name of the Lord Jesus."

"Take time to be holy,

The world rushes on;

Spend much time in secret,

With Jesus alone.

By looking to Jesus,

Like Him thou shalt be,

Thy friends in thy conduct,

His likeness shall see."

Did you love *Collected Writings On ... Exploring Biblical Holiness*? Then you should read *Different Discipleship: Jesus' Sermon on the Mount* by Hayes Press!

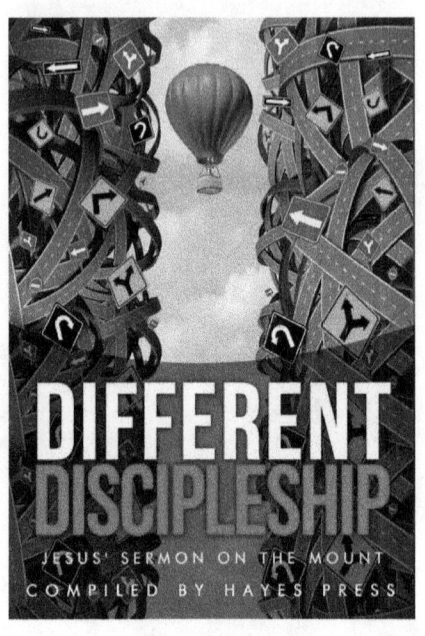

A practical, challenging study (complete with questions and prayer prompts) of the "Sermon on the Mount" for followers and would-be followers of Jesus. What makes Jesus and his followers "different"? Find out why this revolutionary, life-changing sermon is why Jesus Christ is regarded as one of the world's most important teachers, even by those who don't follow him as their Lord and Saviour.

CHAPTER ONE: THE SETTING OF THE SERMON
CHAPTER TWO: HAPPY ARE THE POOR AND

MOURNING
CHAPTER THREE: HAPPY ARE THE MEEK, HUNGRY AND THIRSTY
CHAPTER FOUR: HAPPY ARE THE PERSECUTED
CHAPTER FIVE: LET YOUR LIGHT SHINE
CHAPTER SIX: IN DANGER OF THE HELL OF FIRE
CHAPTER SEVEN: TURN THE OTHER CHEEK
CHAPTER EIGHT: SEEK GOD'S APPROVAL, NOT MAN'S
CHAPTER NINE: YOUR HEART IS WHERE YOUR TREASURE IS
CHAPTER TEN: LOVE YOUR NEIGHBOUR
CHAPTER ELEVEN: CUT DOWN AND THROWN IN THE FIRE
CHAPTER TWELVE: FIRST THINGS FIRST
CHAPTER THIRTEEN: THE TEACHER WITH UNIQUE AUTHORITY

Also by Hayes Press

The Road Through Calvary: 40 Devotional Readings
Lovers of God's House
Different Discipleship: Jesus' Sermon on the Mount
The House of God: Past, Present and Future
The Kingdom of God
Knowing God: His Names and Nature
Needed Truth 1888-1988: A Centenary Review of Major Themes
Churches of God: Their Constitution and Functions
Collected Writings On ... Exploring Biblical Fellowship
Collected Writings On ... Exploring Biblical Hope
Collected Writings On ... The Cross of Christ
Builders for God
Collected Writings On ... Exploring Biblical Faithfulness
Collected Writings On ... Exploring Biblical Joy
Possessing the Land: Spiritual Lessons from Joshua
Collected Writings On ... Exploring Biblical Holiness
Collected Writings On ... Exploring Biblical Faith
Collected Writings On ... Exploring Biblical Love
These Three Remain...Exploring Biblical Faith, Hope and Love
The Teaching and Testimony of the Apostles

Pressure Points - Biblical Advice for 20 of Life's Biggest Challenges

More Than a Saviour: Exploring the Person and Work of Jesus

The Faith: Outlines of Scripture Doctrine

Elders and the Elderhood: In Principle, In Practice

Key Doctrines of the Christian Gospel

Is There a Purpose to Life?

Bible Covenants 101

The Hidden Christ - Volume 2: Offerings and Sacrifices

The Hidden Christ Volume 1: Types and Shadows in the Old Testament

The Hidden Christ - Volume 3: Types and Shadows in Genesis

Heavenly Meanings - The Parable of Jesus

Fisherman to Follower: The Life and Teaching of Simon Peter

About the Publisher

Hayes Press (www.hayespress.org) is a registered charity in the United Kingdom, whose primary mission is to disseminate the Word of God, mainly through literature. It is one of the largest distributors of gospel tracts and leaflets in the United Kingdom, with over 100 titles and hundreds of thousands despatched annually.

Hayes Press also publishes Plus Eagles Wings, a fun and educational Bible magazine for children, and Golden Bells, a popular daily Bible reading calendar in wall or desk formats.

Also available are over 100 Bibles in many different versions, shapes and sizes, Christmas cards, Christian jewellery, Eikos Bible Art, Bible text posters and much more!

www.ingramcontent.com/pod-product-compliance
Lightning Source LLC
Chambersburg PA
CBHW071259040426
42444CB00009B/1790